FOREWORD

Confidence is an element in recovery—not false optimism about world or national recovery but confidence in the ability of a company to succeed in even the most adverse climate.

The abolition of pay, prices, exchange and dividend controls, the progressive withdrawal of government intervention, and successive attacks on bureaucracy leave business performance measurable no longer in macro terms but in the performance of individual companies. The successful companies are usually those who plan ahead.

Needless to say, those who cope well in a recession, positive well-directed companies, will also do best in an expansionary period. It is they who will be poised to capture the share of growing markets during a time when traditionally British companies have lost market share through unpreparedness.

This book also highlights the risks inherent in expansion, not least in cash flow. The Institute of Directors is particularly concerned with the role of the board of Directors during this critical period—the function of direction—challenging the technology of all departments, assessing management strength, setting the employee relations scene, detecting financial vulnerability, ensuring that short-term budgets are consistent with long-term plans and setting standards of service and quality.

I therefore commend this expansion kit to you and suggest that you set up a strategy session away from your normal routine, motivate your board of Directors and your senior executives, and make this book your agenda. Then move to GO!

Walter Goldsmith
Director-General
Institute of Directors
London SW1
February 1983

ACKNOWLEDGEMENTS

Many members of Touche Ross & Co. contributed their ideas and their efforts to this project. In particular, acknowledgement is given to John Roques and Christopher Tanner who took these ideas and efforts and turned them into a book.

CONTENTS

INTRODUCTION

These words are written in the hope that the first signs of the end of Britain's recession are just below the horizon.

A lot of businesses have failed. We hope that the many which remain will replace the challenge of survival with the challenge of expansion. If you are the proprietor or managing director of a successful business, large or small, with the will to grow, this kit will help you.

Your business can expand in many ways including by:

● investing in additional capacity

● exploiting new home markets

● doing business abroad

● acquiring another business

● expanding the product range.

The end of the recession itself will imply growth in demand which could affect you. The precise effects of expansion in your business will be unique. This kit attempts to identify some of the ground rules and prompt ideas on how the various opportunities for expansion should be approached.

Expansion offers risks as well as rewards. Cash shortages, production bottlenecks and human failure are just a few of many common symptoms of an overstretched business. This kit places emphasis on effective management of a growing business. Early in a business's development, management by the seat of the pants can be effective. There comes a point, however, where this won't work any more. We want you to learn the easy way and we have devoted chapters to:

● business objectives and planning

● budgeting and management reporting

● cash forecasting and control.

These themes recur in the rest of the kit. If your business is tightly managed already, then omit the first three chapters but only if you are sure that you have nothing more to learn.

The kit is written to be applicable to all sorts of businesses. Inevitably the examples used may not relate directly to you but we hope that the basic messages will remain. To help you to relate these messages to your own business, each chapter includes a checklist. We recommend that you complete these checklists. This need not take long and even the one or two new ideas which may emerge will reward your effort. The kit is intended to be of broad interest so none of the chapters goes into the subjects in depth. To help you to investigate further we have included in each chapter a section on where to go for further help. These sections suggest organisations to approach and books to read which could help you find the details you need to apply the ideas in this kit to your business.

The kit is not designed as a technical reference work and very little in it is new. We hope, however, that it will provide a framework for you to test your ideas and think through the implications of expansion for your business. That is why we have called it 'Expansion Kit for Business'.

We wish you success with the future growth of your business.

Touche Ross & Co.
London EC4
February 1983

1. BUSINESS OBJECTIVES AND PLANNING

Expansion offers any business a great challenge. Tough decisions have to be made. New products or unfamiliar markets may have to be developed and new skills learned to deal with them. The stakes are high, since the results may be sparkling success or the destruction of the business itself. Why should the act of expansion cause such different results? Every expanding business has its own story, but the common pitfalls are:

● lack of clear objectives

● lack of energetic leadership

● lack of financial knowledge.

These pitfalls have to be avoided but there is a tool which applies to all of them. That tool is planning.

Advantages of planning

Planning does not have to be sophisticated, but it does have to be done. It is one of the most important functions of management and should be done formally. No matter how small your business, formal planning has these advantages:

Discipline.   Planning helps to organise your own thoughts, challenge old ideas and create the climate for new ones.

Direction.   It helps to communicate a positive, 'top-down' management style which will help convince others such as staff, investors and bankers of the direction in which the business is going.

Control.   A benchmark is established against which to monitor the day to day decision making process.

If you have done your planning, then you will be the master of events when the opportunity to expand arrives. Do not wait for the opportunity, plan for it.

Planning summary

Volumes have been written on business planning. The important thing is that it is done. The basic steps are:

● determining the objectives

● identifying strategies

● preparing plans

● evaluating the plans.

These planning steps are explained in greater detail later, but each business must find its own way of applying them in its own circumstances. Here are some basic questions to be answered first, whatever the size of your business:

Who does the planning?   Effective planning needs imagination and the motivation to challenge the status quo. Whoever does it must have these qualities and the credibility in the business to be allowed to see it through. Think this out carefully, since the obvious choices may not be the best. For example, the managing director may not be the best person to challenge the status quo, even though he should be!

Small businesses will have less choice than larger ones but the question still repays thought. A sole trader might, for example, find the objectivity of an outsider useful – a fellow businessman perhaps or the sole trader's accountant.

When and where is the planning done?   Too many businesses allow day-to-day working pressures to interfere with their long-term planning. A sudden opportunity to expand may itself represent a severe pressure. Creative thought, however, requires the right environment and your office is probably not the right place for it. Why not overcome this by arranging important planning sessions out of the office? The change in atmosphere will also help new ideas to emerge more easily.

How far ahead should you plan?   Nobody can predict the future with certainty. Effective action today, however, requires a view on what the future holds and we should not shy away from this. All businesses should have a detailed plan of the year ahead together with an outline plan for the longer term. The length of the longer-term plan will depend on your business but three years will usually suffice.

Determining the objectives

Why are you in business? How rich do you want to be?

Many businessmen never ask themselves these questions, let alone answer them. If you do, your company will have more sense of direction than the competition. Here are some tips to help you:

Find out what the proprietors want.   This is easier than it sounds. It will depend on factors such as the age, attitudes and wealth of the proprietors. A sole trader will only have himself to consider whilst a family company may have conflicting interests to reconcile. Typical factors in formulating objectives include profit, security of investment or employment, influence, provision of a service in a particular field and a stimulating working environment. A young entrepreneur might put more emphasis on profit whilst a doctor might be more concerned with service, for example.

This book is about expansion. Is growth one of your objectives? Challenge yourself carefully on this since the answer is likely to be no! For most businesses expansion is a means of achieving an objective, such as more profit, not an objective in itself.

Set a profit target.   Most businesses want to make a profit, but how much? 'As much as possible' is the usual answer!

In fact this is rarely true. An example is a sole trader who feels content with his profit if it provides a comfortable living for his family and allows him the time to work in local politics. A professional practice which prefers not to deal with dubious clients is another!

There is a further aspect to this. Many businesses use the budgeting process to prepare a 'target'. This is the wrong way round! Strongly-managed companies decide on the profit target first and require budgets to be prepared to meet it. In a group of companies the overall profit target should be broken down and each company given its own target to meet.

Determine the amount of profit the proprietors would find acceptable for each year to be covered by the plans. This should be the basis for your targets.

Document the objectives and targets.   The discipline of documenting your conclusions will help you to get them right and gain the commitment of others. Write from the proprietors' point of view; be brief and precise.

Identifying strategies

The next step is to write a brief statement of the alternative actions the business could take to achieve the objectives and profit target. These are your potential strategies. It might turn out that no important changes are needed, although this is unlikely. A good way of tackling this systematically is to start by reviewing the status quo:

Analyse the environment.   Review the environment in which your business operates and identify the significant factors. Typically, these will include economic, legal and technological factors. The impact of new scientific developments on the competitiveness of your products is an example of the last of these factors. The effect of taxation on your profits is an example of the second.

Analyse your business.   Try to identify the existing strengths and weaknesses of your business. You should review your products, marketing, organisation and administration, people and finance. For example, one of your business's strengths may be a well-known brand name whilst a weakness may be overdependence upon one product.

Identify the constraints.   Constraints may arise for a host of reasons: legal, moral, economic, safety, union influence and so on. One company might not wish to consider making components for armaments, for example, whilst another might not inconvenience staff by relocating. Review each of your business areas and be ruthless in identifying what the constraints of your own business are.

A thorough analysis of the possible strategies should follow. These will be specific to each of your business areas but might include the following categories:

- exploiting new home markets for existing products
- exporting
- diversifying
- integrating
- acquiring another business
- capital investment
- discontinuing
- improving profit through marketing and cost-cutting
- tax planning.

Guidance on strategies for expansion is the subject of much of this book. Having completed your review, write a concise statement of the strategies available to your business. Expansion may be one of these!

Preparing plans

The next step is to select the strategies to be applied during the planning period and prepare a detailed action plan for their execution. The detailed action plan should consist of a concisely written report of what the business is going to do. Here are some suggested headings and what they might cover. Under each heading, you should identify who is responsible for executing each aspect of the plan and by when:

Environment.   A brief statement of the overall assumptions on which the plan is based.

Product plan.   A description of each product and how its production will be achieved.

Marketing plan.   A clear statement of marketing objectives, including details of pricing, projected sales, advertising and outlets for each product.

Organisation and administration plan. Details of how the organisation will have to change to reflect the development of the business. This will include information systems, reporting structures and internal control. This is particularly important if the business is expanding through multi-locations or products, or doing business abroad for the first time. The need for timely management information in these circumstances may require more staff or perhaps computerisation.

People plan. Even modest expansion plans cannot be achieved without the right people and yet many plans fail because this is overlooked. The plan should set out the skills required together with plans for promotion, training and recruitment. Do not assume however, that this is enough. People need motivation to perform well and this should be planned too.

Finance plan. Expansion needs finance. The plan will include appraisal of proposed capital investment, cash requirements, sources of finance and taxation.

Evaluating the plans

The final link is to confirm that the plans meet the objectives and profit target.

This step can be tedious but it is vital. You should prepare profit and cash flow forecasts for one year in detail and three years in outline. The techniques for doing this are given in Chapters 2 and 3.

Does your plan meet your objectives? This book assumes that it does and that a major strategy is expansion. How to make that expansion happen is the subject of the rest of this book.

A planning checklist

1. Give business planning the priority it deserves by:

    ● identifying the right people to do it ☐

    ● establishing an annual planning timetable ☐

    ● selecting an appropriate venue. ☐

2. Select a planning horizon which is suitable for the business, but not less than three years. ☐

3. Write down the proprietors' business objectives and profit targets and review them annually. ☐

4. Perform a thorough review of the business and identify all the potential strategies available having regard to the constraints. ☐

5. Select the business strategies for your business and prepare a detailed plan for their execution over the planning period. Review the plans annually and extend them for another year. □

6. Evaluate the plans by preparing profit and cash flow forecasts and comparing them with profit targets. □

7. Identify who is responsible for executing each aspect of the plan and by when and monitor that person's performance. □

8. Remember that expansion is one of the possible consequences of good planning but is not the reason for it. □

Further action to be taken by me

1.

2.

3.

4.

5.

6.

Where to go for further help

Organisations

Association of British Chambers of Commerce
Sovereign House, 212 Shaftesbury Avenue, London WC2H 8EW
Tel: 01-240 5831

Association of Independent Businesses
Trowbray House, 108 Weston St., London SE1 3QB
Tel: 01-403 4066

British Institute of Management
Management House, Parker St., London WC2B 5PT
Tel: 01-405 3456

Confederation of British Industry
Centre Point, 103 New Oxford St., London WC1A 1DU
Tel: 01-379 7400

Council for Small Industries in Rural Areas (CoSIRA)
141 Castle St., Salisbury, Wilts. SP1 3TP
Tel: 0722 6255

Department of Industry, Small Firms Centres
(Regional Offices)
Freefone 2444

Institute of Management Consultants
23-24 Cromwell Place, London SW7 2LG
Tel: 01-584 7285

London Chamber of Commerce and Industry
69-73 Cannon St., London EC4N 5AB
Tel: 01-248 4444

National Enterprise Board
101 Newington Causeway, London SE1 6EU
Tel: 01-403 6666

National Federation of Self-Employed and Small Businesses
32 St. Annes Road West, Lytham St. Annes, Lancs. FY8 1NY
Tel: 0253 720911

Small Business Bureau
32 Smith Square, London SW1P 3HH
Tel: 01-222 9000 (ext 2208)

Books

A Practical Approach to Financial Management, J Gibbs, Financial Training Publications (2nd ed)

Financial Management Handbook, Kluwer: Part 1 Formulating the Plan

Practical Corporate Planning, J Argenti, George Allen & Unwin (1980)

Successful Business Policies, G D Newbould and G A Luffman, Gower (1978)

The Complete Guide to Managing Your Business, Eaglemoss: Ch 2 Financial Planning and Management

Tolley's Survival Kit for Small Businesses, Touche Ross & Co, Tolley (1981): Ch 9 Business Planning

2. BUDGETING AND MANAGEMENT REPORTING

Your expansion plans need more than pious hopes for their success. The first essential is the commitment of top management who must provide the leadership. They will have been involved in the planning process and so will know the direction the business is taking.

A sense of direction at the top, however, is not enough without the support of all the staff. It is easy for management to forget, even in small companies, that staff will not know what is happening if nobody informs them. This is a very common problem. Typical symptoms of this kind of management which emerge amongst the staff are:

● lack of initiative

● constant raising of minor issues at too senior a level

● criticism of management

● low morale

● resignations of the best staff

● gossip.

Expansion usually leads to a reduction in the personal contact between managers and their staff and it is then that these symptoms often arise. This is one of many good reasons for establishing a reliable budgeting and management reporting system.

Budgeting

Your business planning will have identified the profit target and the action plans (see Chapter 1). The budget is simply the annual action plan expressed in money. The budgeting process helps the communication of the management's intentions to the staff and provides a benchmark against which actual performance can be monitored. The budget statements should be designed to:

● include an overall profit and loss account, cash flow forecast and balance sheet

● enable the results of distinct operations to be measured – each operation will probably need separate budgets for sales, production costs and overheads

● reflect the frequency with which the results will be monitored e.g. monthly

- show sufficient detail to allow significant variations from budget to be identified
- be compatible with the management reporting system
- avoid any confusion of responsibility for each section of the budget
- meet the profit targets determined by management.

Here are some common questions about budgeting procedures generally. (In the next chapter cash budgeting is dealt with in greater detail.)

When are budgets prepared?   It is important to complete the budget before the financial year begins. This applies even though the actual results of the previous year will not be known precisely. If this is not done, the discipline of performance measurement will lapse in the first months of the year. If the monthly reporting procedures described later are in operation then the production of the annual accounts should not give rise to any surprises.

Should budgets be revised?   The short answer is no. In practice, actual results always vary from budget. There is nothing surprising about this. One function of the budget is to provide a benchmark from which deviations from the plan can be monitored. If the benchmark is constantly changed, then deviations from the plan will be disguised and confusion will result. If, however, a budget contains errors so serious that the credibility of the whole system is threatened, then a change may be necessary. You should be worried if budget changes are common in your business.

Who prepares the budget?   As your business expands, so you will need to develop an effective second tier of management which will take responsibility for segments or departments of the business. An effective way of gaining its commitment to the business plans is to involve the second tier in the budgeting process. If a budget, which has been prepared by a manager, is accepted by senior management then the manager's commitment to meet it will be obtained. In negotiating acceptance of the budget, it is important to maintain a balance between the need for profit or growth and your manager's belief in what is possible.

One mistake to avoid is delegating the whole budgeting process to an accountant. Other managers will quickly wash their hands of budgets imposed on them in this way. An accountant should, of course, be involved in preparing any budget for which he is directly responsible. He will probably also be the right man to co-ordinate the efforts of others such as the sales or production managers. An effective accountant should also provide a useful challenge to the budgets by giving them a detailed review.

How should budgets be prepared?   The past is often the best guide to the future and, in practice, the budgeting process will normally start with last year's achievements. The figures will then be adjusted to reflect planned changes. Even in a stable business, adjustments will have to be made for inflation, expected wage settlements and changing interest rates.

The main weakness of this approach is perpetuating the mistakes of the past. For an expanding business these mistakes can be multiplied. It is a good idea to attempt periodically to prepare budgets from 'square one'. This technique is known as 'zero-based budgeting' and is a useful device for examining the business objectively and questioning established practices. If you have ambitious expansion plans, then zero-based budgets may be the best alternative.

How should shared services be treated?   Where costs borne centrally can be controlled by departmental managers, they should be allocated to departmental budgets. These may include interest costs and perhaps stationery, printing and maintenance and other costs of this sort.

The allocation of other central costs can give a broad sense of overall profitability, but arbitrary allocations may lead to pointless debate about the bases and divert attention from important questions such as whether the cost should be incurred at all.

In any event if costs are allocated it is important that someone should be responsible for budgeting them centrally and then controlling the actual costs against these budgets. Departmental managers will resent the allocation of costs to them which they feel are not subjected to the same disciplines as their own.

Management reporting

Management reporting is often assumed to be a sophisticated affair suitable only for large businesses. This is not the case. Every businessman needs to make decisions and size is no excuse for making them without the right information. Every business should identify the information which it needs to enable it to make effective decisions and then design a management reporting system to provide it.

If the business is simple, the management reporting package will be simple.

All businesses need to know on a regular basis the:

● profitability of each operation
● order position
● ability to meet orders from stock or anticipated deliveries
● cash requirements

13

● credit risks

● capacity of the business to accept further business.

Most businesses need this information monthly. The management reporting package must be designed to provide it. The proprietors, or in larger businesses the senior management team, must set time aside each month to review it. A great deal of time will be saved if the management reporting package shows clearly the actual results for the month with the budgeted amount alongside. This means that the management's time is directed towards reviewing the important deviations from plan. A typical monthly profit and loss account is shown in Fig 2.1 as an example of the way in which information can be presented.

How are management reports prepared?   Your accountant's primary task is to give you the information you need and he should establish a suitable recording system to do this efficiently.

One of the most important management reports is the profit and loss account. Every business must keep a record of sales made and this is the starting point for the monthly profit and loss account.

The next step is to establish the cost of the resources which have been consumed in making the sales. These are often called direct costs. These will usually consist of materials and production labour costs. In some businesses it is possible to identify direct costs for each sale but in others this may not be practicable. In that case it will be necessary to rely on a standard gross margin to compute the direct costs.

The value of sales less the direct costs gives the sales contribution. To determine the profit it is then only necessary to deduct the overheads. Salaries, depreciation and recurring costs such as rent and rates are easy to establish. Other overheads may have to be estimated until invoices are received.

When are management reports prepared?   As soon as possible. It is important to maintain a balance between the timeliness of the reports and reasonable accuracy. Highly accurate figures which arrive too late are useless. Estimates of many figures are often sufficient. In some profit centres comparatively few figures are really significant.

Fig 2.1   Profit and loss account—Pro-forma

Note.   The profit and loss account should be designed specifically to suit your business. There is no single correct format but keep it simple. You must decide whether to show explanations of variances from budget, important ratios and further analysis in separate schedules or include them on the face of the account.

Fig 2.1   Profit and loss account—Pro-forma continued

Profit and loss account for month A of 198X

	Month			Cumulative for year to date		
	Actual	Budget	Prior Year	Actual	Budget	Prior Year
	£	£	£	£	£	£
Sales						
Product A						
B						
C						
Direct Costs						
Product A						
B						
C						
Contribution						
Product A						
B						
C						
Overheads						
Factory						
Sales						
Administration						
Finance costs						
Net profit						

How and when are the estimates verified? It is important that estimates are verified from time to time and certainly more regularly than by annual audit. Many poor estimates will become apparent from reviewing the management reports themselves whilst others will be corrected the following month when more facts are known, e.g. an invoice arrives.

The main difficulty arises where an estimated gross profit margin is used. The key to verification here is to prepare a balance sheet. Estimate this monthly so that if the stock figures seem unrealistically high, you can consider whether this suggests that your gross margins are overstated. Finally, perhaps quarterly, or at least half yearly, count and value the stock to prove the accuracy of the information you have been using.

Comparison with budgets. The process of comparing the monthly results with the budget amounts to the appraisal of the success or failure of your performance in implementing the plans. Do not, however, waste management time explaining every small difference that arises every month. Trends must be observed and explanations obtained for continuing variations. Remember that the purpose of the comparison is not to amuse your company accountant but to enable management to identify action that is required to maintain or improve business performance. This is the purpose of management reporting systems. If they do not assist the decision making processes, then either the system or the management must be changed.

A budgeting and management reporting checklist

1. Identify the information which you need on a regular basis to make effective decisions. Design the simplest management reporting package which is capable of providing this information and to show clearly variations from budget. ☐

2. Establish a timetable for the production and review of the management reporting package. Timeliness is more important than excessive accuracy. ☐

3. Ensure that the action plans are clearly communicated to your staff and involve them in the budgeting and reporting process. ☐

4. Establish annual budgets before the financial year begins and avoid unnecessary revision thereafter. ☐

5. Challenge the assumption when budgeting that the future will be the same as to the past. ☐

6. Avoid arbitrary or unnecessary allocation of shared costs to departmental budgets. ☐

16

7. Use sound financial control to minimise the risks accompanying expansion. ☐

Further action to be taken by me

1.

2.

3.

4.

5.

6.

Where to go for further help

Organisations. The best person to contact is almost certainly your accountant.

Books

Accounting and Finance, F Wood and J Hellings, Polytech Publishers (1970)

Accounting in Business, R J Bull, Butterworth (4th ed, 1980)

An Insight into Management Accounting, J Sizer, Pelican Books (1980): Ch 9 Budgetary planning and control systems

Financial Management Handbook, Kluwer: 6.1 Budgetary control systems

Handbook of Financial Planning and Control, M A Pocock and A H Taylor (editors), Gower (1981): Ch 4 Income and expenditure budgets, Ch 5 Capital budgeting, and Ch 7 Assessment of performance

Introduction to Management Accounting, C T Horngren, Prentice-Hall International (5th ed, 1981, previously Accounting for Management Control)

Management Accountancy, J Batty, Macdonald and Evans (5th ed due November 1982)

Management Accounting Systems and Records, B Grimsley, Gower (2nd ed, 1982)

Managing Your Company's Finances, R Hargreaves and R Smith, Heinemann (1981)

Tolley's Survival Kit for Small Businesses, Touche Ross & Co, Tolley (1981): Ch 10 Costing and budgetary control

3. CASH FORECASTING AND CONTROL

The plan for your expansion will fail if your cash runs out. This apparently simple fact is ignored too often, sometimes with disastrous results. The lure of the profits which expansion may bring can even colour the judgment of normally prudent businessmen. Profit and cash are not the same thing, however, and expansion will emphasise this. For example:

● growth in sales tends to increase stock and debtors

● investment in plant or products has an immediate impact on cash but a long-term effect on profit

● overheads may have to increase ahead of planned increases in sales volume.

These are just some of the possible factors likely to effect the cash needs of your expansion plans. It is a vital part of your planning to complete the list of factors for your business and evaluate the effect by preparing a long-term cash forecast and a short-term cash budget.

Long-term cash forecasting

Your business plan will include a long-term profit forecast (see Chapter 1). This can be used as the basis for preparing a simple long-term cash budget. The idea is to:

● identify and evaluate non-cash items included in the projected profit and loss account, for example, depreciation, provisions and additional working capital requirements

● adjust the projected profit to effect the differences identified

● determine projected capital expenditure, profit distribution and taxation payments and enter these on the forecast.

The most difficult figure to identify accurately is likely to be the additional working capital requirement.

The method is illustrated in Fig 3.1 by an example of a small, but rapidly expanding, business.

The long-term cash forecast prepared in this way will identify any fundamental cash constraints implied by the plans and indicate the trend of financing needs. It is thus essentially a planning tool. In Fig 3.1, the business has to be able to finance an outflow of cash by year 3 of £23,000. This is in addition to loans and a capital injection already planned totalling £45,000. It would be foolhardy to embark on the expansion without knowing that finance will be available, no matter how attractive the growth in profits might be. Planning your long-term cash position and keeping your bank manager informed of progress will do a lot to build your bank manager's confidence in you.

Short-term cash budgeting

The first step in controlling cash is to prepare a cash budget. This should be done at the same time as the profit budget. The principles of sound budgeting were outlined in the previous chapter but they are just as relevant here. The budgeting process helps the communication of the management's intentions to the staff and provides a benchmark against which actual performance can be monitored.

The method used to prepare the long-term cash forecast will only be suitable for the short-term budget if:

- the long-term cash forecast shows a comfortable surplus

- there are no significant peaks or troughs in business activity throughout the year

- you have a track record of accurate cash forecasting

- internal controls over cash are strong

- no fundamental change in the business is anticipated.

Fig 3.1   Longer-term cash flow forecast—Example

Note 1.   The depreciation charge in your profit forecast reduces the profit but does not reduce the cash. It must therefore be added back to profit to calculate the cash inflow. There may be other non-cash items such as provisions on contracts or lease amortisation which you must also add back.

Note 2.   Capital expenditure will be supported by a more detailed budget where appropriate.

Note 3.   The working capital adjustment is crucial. Expansion and inflation are both cash traps, locking up working capital in debtors and stock. Contraction can release cash but this is not always the case. For example, in some cash-sale businesses, where your suppliers compete for your trade by allowing you extended credit, contraction can limit cash flow.

Business can be disrupted by industrial disputes in a major customer or supplier, by the illness of key staff, or by failure of a piece of equipment. These storms can be ridden out with adequate finance to retain staff, manufacture stock or whatever. The inclusion of a contingency to cover such disruptions should be considered.

Note 4.   The forecast for Year 1 will be supported in detail by the short-term cash-flow budget.

Fig 3.1   Longer-term cash flow forecast—Example continued

	Note	Year 1 £'000	Year 2 £'000	Year 3 £'000
Turnover (memo only)		100	150	320
Receipts				
Pre-tax profits, per profits forecast		10	15	40
Add back non-cash items:	1			
Depreciation		5	7	10
(Profit)/loss on disposal of assets		—	(1)	—
Other		—	—	—
Proceeds of disposal of assets		—	4	—
Total cash in (A)		15	25	50
Payments				
Capital expenditure	2	22	12	15
Profit distribution		—	1	2
Taxation		—	2	15
Additional working capital requirements:	3			
Stock increase		2	8	20
Receivables increase		2	10	40
Contingency		2	5	5
Less increased use of creditors' funds		(1)	(8)	(15)
Total cash out (B)		27	30	82
Funding summary				
Opening cash balance/(overdraft)		(10)	(14)	(16)
Net outflow (B-A)		(12)	(5)	(32)
Net inflow (A-B)		—	—	—
Loans already planned		10	5	15
Loans repayments		(2)	(2)	(5)
Additional capital injections		—	—	15
Closing cash balance/(overdraft)	4	(14)	(16)	(23)

It is unlikely that all these will apply to an expanding business, so another method is needed. Fig 3.2 illustrates a suitable layout for a short-term cash budget and below are set out some tips for completing it for your own business.

(Do not forget to reconcile the short-term cash budget with the long-term cash forecast.)

Receipts.   Analyse your sales budget for the next year over each of the twelve months.

Distinguish between cash and credit sales. Cash sales should be included in the pro-forma in the month of sale; credit sales in the month when the customer will probably pay. Beware of payments on account. Include VAT in sales if significant.

Include any irregular receipts such as tax refunds or sales of fixed assets.

Trading payments.   Analyse your likely purchases of materials over the next twelve months on a separate sheet. Distinguish between cash and credit purchases. Cash purchases should be included in the pro-forma in the month of purchase; credit purchases in the month when payment will be made. Watch out for major payments on account and other unusual payments.

Enter gross wages and salaries plus employers' NIC.

Overhead payments.   Itemise all major cost elements.

Forecast cash outgoings for the period, taking care with quarterly, half-yearly or annual items such as rent, rates, insurance and pension premiums, loan interest, etc.

Enter the appropriate amounts in the month when payments will be made. This is not necessarily when they will become due.

Include all other overheads on an average basis, i.e. one-twelfth for each month.

Other items.   Enter capital purchases in the months when payment will be made. Do not forget long-delivery items ordered months ago.

Record all dividend payments and other profit distributions together with any advance corporation tax arising on such distributions.

Do not forget other taxation payments (other than PAYE), including VAT if significant.

Loan repayments must include those stated in your expansion plans.

Other payments will be particular to your own business and plans. Removal expenses or the cost of a marketing campaign are examples.

Cash reporting

Cash is the life blood of a business. The top management should be involved in monitoring it to ensure that its utilisation is effective. The reports required are:

* a daily summary of the cash position in both the business and the bank's records (likely to be different because of uncleared items)
* a daily summary of surplus cash available
* a bank reconciliation at least monthly
* a monthly comparison of the actual cash position with budget as part of the management reporting package.

Differences arising from the last comparison are most important. Whereas differences between the actual and budgeted profit require explanation but only sometimes action, differences between the actual and budgeted cash position almost always require action. Firstly, you must establish whether the difference is a temporary one due to timing or a permanent change. In the latter case, the year's cash forecast must be recalculated, taking account of the new circumstances. Action must then be taken to reduce the net outflow, so that margins between balance and overdraft limit are maintained and, exceptionally, plans made to invest a surplus. This review and any resulting action must not be delayed, since the more time you have before limits are reached, the more likely it is that these problems can be resolved.

Speeding up cash receipts

There are steps that can be taken to improve cash flow and the most obvious place to start is with the company's sales. The typical separate steps in a sales cycle are:

* order received from customer
* credit controller investigates and authorises sale
* production
* warehouse assembles goods for despatch
* goods despatched to customer
* accounts department prepares invoice
* invoice posted
* customer receives invoice and passes it through his own accounting systems
* customer prepares cheque and posts it

Fig 3.2   Short-term cash budget. Amounts in thousands of pounds.

	Jan	Feb	Mar	Apr	May
Receipts					
Cash sales	800	1,000	1,000	1,000	1,000
From debtors	7,500	6,000	5,000	6,000	6,750
Tax refunds	—	—	—	—	—
Other sources	10,000	—	—	—	—
Total A	18,300	7,000	6,000	7,000	7,750
Payments					
Trading					
Cash purchases	100	100	100	100	100
To creditors	7,200	4,300	3,700	3,500	3,700
Wages and salaries	1,200	1,200	1,200	1,200	1,200
Other payments	170	170	160	170	170
Overheads					
Rent, rates, water	400	400	400	1,400	400
Insurance	600	—	150	—	—
Light, heat, power	—	750	—	—	550
Repairs and renewals	100	100	100	100	100
HP and leasing payments	—	—	—	—	—
Bank charges and interest	30	30	410	30	30
Telephone and postage	50	50	200	50	50
Other payments	20	20	20	20	20
Other Items					
Purchase of fixed assets	—	—	—	12,000	—
Dividends	—	—	—	—	—
Tax payments	—	—	—	—	—
Drawings, fees	—	—	—	—	—
Loan repayments	—	—	500	—	—
Other payments	—	—	—	—	—
Total B	9,870	7,120	6,940	18,570	6,320
Net inflow (A-B)/ outflow (B-A)	8,430	(120)	(940)	(11,570)	1,430
Balance brought forward	(10,000)	(1,570)	(1,690)	(2,630)	(14,200)
Balance carried forward	(1,570)	(1,690)	(2,630)	(14,200)	(12,770)

Jun	Jul	Aug	Sep	Oct	Nov	Dec	Total
900	750	900	1,250	1,400	1,500	1,500	13,000
7,250	6,000	5,500	5,000	9,200	10,300	10,500	85,000
—	—	—	—	—	—	—	—
—	—	—	—	—	—	—	10,000
8,150	6,750	6,400	6,250	10,600	11,800	12,000	108,000
100	100	100	100	100	100	100	1,200
3,600	3,300	3,200	3,300	5,200	5,700	6,700	53,400
1,200	1,200	1,400	1,500	1,600	1,600	1,900	16,400
160	170	170	160	170	170	160	2,000
400	400	400	400	1,400	400	400	6,800
—	100	—	150	—	—	—	1,000
—	—	650	—	—	850	—	2,800
100	100	100	100	100	100	100	1,200
—	—	—	—	—	—	—	—
390	30	30	370	30	30	350	1,760
200	50	50	200	50	50	200	1,200
20	20	20	20	20	20	20	240
—	—	5,000	—	—	5,000	—	22,000
—	—	—	—	—	—	—	—
—	—	—	—	—	—	—	—
—	—	—	—	—	—	—	—
500	—	—	500	—	—	500	2,000
—	—	—	—	—	—	—	—
6,670	5,470	11,120	6,800	8,670	14,020	10,430	112,000
1,480	1,280	(4,720)	(550)	1,930	(2,220)	1,570	(4,000)
(12,770)	(11,290)	(10,010)	(14,730)	(15,280)	(13,350)	(15,570)	(10,000)
(11,290)	(10,010)	(14,730)	(15,280)	(13,350)	(15,570)	(14,000)	(14,000)

- cheque received
- cheque banked
- bank clears cheque
- business has cash available in its bank.

The company must review its system, determine the amount of time taken by each of these separate stages and determine where improvements can be made.

Most successful businesses deal well with the steps up to the point where goods are despatched to the customer. If this were not so orders would be lost. It is common however not to pay enough attention to controlling the related paperwork with the result that invoicing and collections are unnecessarily delayed.

Invoicing. Most companies hope that their sales invoices will be paid within 30 days. In practice, many are not paid until 50-60 days after the invoice date. Speed is critical and you should be sure to invoice as quickly as possible after a sale is made. Do not wait until the end of the month, particularly if the sale is for a large amount. Consider part deliveries and invoicing each separately. Check that your invoices are easy to understand and that all the relevant information such as order numbers, quantities, descriptions, part numbers, unit prices, extensions and additions are accurate. An invoice which is inaccurate gives your customer an excuse to delay payment.

Sales discounts. Consider introducing discounts for quick payments. Typically, a two per cent discount would be given for payment within ten days, reverting to the normal 30 days credit thereafter. In theory, the company is accepting two per cent less than the sales amount in exchange for the use of the money for 20 days. This translates to an effective annual interest rate of 37%. In practice, most companies take 50-60 days to pay invoices, so, in fact, the discount will give the company use of the money for 40-50 days. This is an effective annual interest rate of between 15% and 18%.

Another alternative is to offer a discount for cash with the order or on delivery. This method is particularly suitable for small orders where both you and your customer can also benefit by simplifying the paperwork.

There are disadvantages to sales discounts. Some customers will take the discount without paying within the discount period. The cost of collecting unearned discounts from customers and the loss of goodwill caused by this may outweigh the advantages. Each company must evaluate its own position.

Credit control.   It is no good invoicing promptly if the customer cannot, or will not, pay. Review your credit control procedures and consider employing a specialist if necessary. Remember that credit control should start before a sale is made and your system should ensure that sales are only made to approved customers, within predetermined credit limits and on confirmed orders.

Once the sale has been made, your system should automatically ensure that payment is chased. Personal contact is the most effective method, usually by telephone, but many customers demand statements before they will pay so you should consider a monthly procedure for this.

Senior management should be made aware of the outstanding collections through the management reporting package (see Chapter 2). A summary of the total amount outstanding, analysed by month, should be included together with a summary of previous months to show the trends. The problematic accounts should be clearly identified, together with a summary of the action which has been taken.

If you do not have the internal resources to chase your debtors effectively consider appointing an external collection agency. This can be linked with raising finance by either factoring your debts or by raising money using your debtors as security.

Clearing receipts.   Ensure that receipts are banked at least daily. Consider introducing direct debits or standing orders for regular customers.

Delaying cash payments

Another way of improving your cash position is by delaying payment. The general policy should be not to pay until you have to but this will be affected by:

- sales terms
- competitive conditions
- discounts available
- relationships with suppliers.

Obviously, a business should not delay payment to the extent that it risks legal action, the wrath or future lack of co-operation of its suppliers, its switchboard being jammed with calls from creditors, or its accountant being tied up answering queries. Nevertheless, delayed payment does conserve a company's cash. Terms of 'net within 30 days' can very often be extended to 60 days and this is probably the period of credit the supplier really expects to have to give. If you do decide to pay late, then it is as well to do it regularly so that your suppliers are not encouraged to panic.

You should also consider the effect of discounts. If the effective interest rate for paying within the discount period is less than the cost of borrowing you should delay payment and not take the discount. On the other hand, if the effective interest rate exceeds the cost of borrowing, then the payment should be made early and the discount taken.

Cash is the key

Businesses only fail when they run out of cash, not necessarily when they run out of orders or incur losses. If you see disaster ahead, do not sit and hope. Reduce your investment in stocks even if sales have to be made at a loss, cut costs that give rise to immediate cash savings and by planning avoid being taken by surprise.

A cash forecasting and control checklist

1. Every year complete:

    ● a long-term cash forecast ☐

    ● a short-term cash budget. ☐

2. Keep your bank manager informed of your progress and your plans. Apply to him for new finance well in advance. ☐

3. Establish an effective cash reporting system including:

    ● a daily cash report including surplus cash available ☐

    ● a monthly bank reconciliation ☐

    ● a monthly comparison of actual cash against budget. ☐

4. Review your sales system and identify ways of speeding up cash receipts particularly by:

    ● efficient invoicing procedures ☐

    ● offering sales and cash discounts ☐

    ● effective credit control ☐

    ● prompt banking of remittances. ☐

5. Review your policy for payments and see if they can be delayed. ☐

Further action to be taken by me

1.

2.

3.

4.

5.

6.

Where to go for further help

Organisations.   The best people to contact are your accountant and your bank manager.

Books

A Practical Approach to Financial Management, J Gibbs, Financial Training Publications (2nd ed, 1980): Ch 2 Cash Flow and Liquidity

Business Finance, B Ogley, Longman (1982)

Cash Flow Management, J E Smith, Woodhead-Faulkner (2nd ed, 1980)

Credit Management, R M V Bass, Business Books (1979)

Credit Management – A survey of credit control and debt collection policies and practice, S Goddard and S Jay, Management Survey Report No 52, 1981, British Institute of Management

Financial Management and Policy, J Van Horne, Prentice-Hall International (5th ed, 1980)

Management of Company Finance, Samuels and Wilkes, Van Nostrand Reinhold (3rd ed, 1980, previously published by Nelson)

Managing Your Company's Finances, R Hargreaves and R Smith, Heinemann (1981)

Tolley's Survival Kit For Small Businesses, Touche Ross & Co, Tolley (1981): Ch 11 Cash Management, and Ch 12 Cash Forecasting

4. CAPITAL INVESTMENT APPRAISAL AND GOVERNMENT INCENTIVES

Expansion usually means capital investment. Should we replace our old plant? Would it be better to lease or buy? All these are capital investment appraisal decisions. They are important aspects of the planning process and should not be considered in isolation from it.

Many factors affect investment decisions including:

● initial outlay

● timing of the cash benefits

● cost of finance

● tax

● government grants.

These factors should be quantified before undertaking the investment. Later in this chapter we show how this might be done.

The risk of technical obsolescence, location, safety and employee preference cannot be quantified so easily. The subjectivity of these factors illustrates that capital investment decisions ultimately involve judgment. The numerical data merely provide one aspect of the information on which the judgment is made. Set out your capital expenditure proposals clearly to show both the financial and the qualitative factors.

If the plans for your business involve capital investment, remember that the government may help you to pay for it! Successive governments in the UK have intervened in the economy to promote capital investment, particularly in manufacturing industry. Each has meddled with what went before, producing a tangled web of legislation which even civil servants do not always understand! Do not be put off. Many of the schemes are generous and may apply to you. Broadly speaking, the main government incentives for investment fall into the categories below:

● tax reliefs

● grants

● enterprise zones

● finance.

Of these, the most important and widely available are tax reliefs.

Note that the above are not the only government incentives but are those which are the most relevant to investment.

A very brief outline of each of the above follows. If in doubt, consult an expert.

Tax reliefs

Many types of capital expenditure will reduce your tax bill. The deductions from your profit which achieve this are called capital allowances. There are several types of allowance and a brief explanation of these is given below. Fig 4.1 also gives details.

Plant and machinery. On the purchase of plant and machinery, a first year allowance is given, amounting to 100% of its cost. The term 'plant and machinery' covers a wide range of items, in addition to plant associated with a factory or workshop. It can include, for example, builders' fixtures and fittings such as boilers, central heating systems, lifts, wash-basins and sanitary ware, moveable partitions, etc., which would normally be thought of as part of a building rather than plant.

Motor vehicles. These are treated as plant except that saloon cars only qualify for a 25% writing down allowance per year, with a maximum of £2,000 per annum for any one car.

Industrial buildings and small workshops. Expenditure on industrial premises qualifies for industrial building allowances. A 75% initial allowance is given in the first year and a 4% writing down allowance in the first and subsequent years. These allowances apply only to new unused industrial buildings, second-hand buildings are treated differently. Small industrial buildings or workshops, with a floor area of no more than 2,500 sq ft qualify for a 100% initial allowance in the first year, up to 26 March 1983. For the following two years, buildings of only up to 1,250 sq ft will qualify.

Commercial buildings such as shops and offices do not qualify for any tax relief whatsoever, except to the extent that the expenditure may be classified as expenditure on plant. An exception is made for commercial buildings in enterprise zones (see below).

The value of tax relief. The value of available tax relief on capital assets depends on whether or not the purchaser is paying tax, and at what rate. The normal rate of tax for a company making profits of over £225,000 is 52%. If profits are £90,000 or below, then the rate may only be 40%. Between £90,000 and £225,000, the effective rate is 60% on the amount over £90,000. For an individual, the rate can be as high as 75%.

If tax is not being paid, then consideration should be given to leasing or renting assets rather than buying. Plant leasing is a very competitive

Fig 4.1   Schedule of capital allowances

	First year	Subsequent years
Plant and machinery	100%	—
Saloon cars	—	25% (max £2,000 p.a.)
Industrial buildings	75%	4%
Small workshops	100%	—
Agriculture and forestry	20%	10%
Scientific research	100%	—

Note.   This table is illustrative of the main capital allowances available but for clarity it has been simplified. The law relating to capital allowances is complex and you should always consult your professional advisers before making any significant investment which may qualify.

market and the lessor tends to pass the value of any tax allowances back to the lessee through a reduced rental charge. This can make plant leasing particularly attractive to the non-taxpayer.

Plant may be bought on hire-purchase rather than outright. The full cash price qualifies for tax relief as soon as the first instalment is paid, provided the plant is then used in the business.

Grants

There are two main types of grant:

Regional Development Grants.   Some areas of the country have been identified as areas where expansion is to be encouraged. These are called Assisted Areas. In these areas capital expenditure on plant, machinery and buildings for many types of manufacturing activities are eligible for grants. The grants are automatic and vary from 15% to 22%, depending on location. They are not taxable.

Selective Financial Assistance.   The objective of Selective Financial Assistance is to enable the government to give aid on a discretionary basis where desirable. Unlike Regional Development Grants, assistance is not restricted to the Assisted Areas. The assistance usually takes the form of a grant and the amount is negotiated individually. The grants are taxable.

Assistance may be provided to:

- promote the development, modernisation or efficiency of an industry
- create, expand or sustain production capacity
- promote the reorganisation of industry.

Remember that to qualify you must be in discussion with the Department of Industry before you start the project. If you believe your project is of benefit to the UK economy, then consider applying. Obtain details on how to apply from your local Department of Industry office.

Enterprise zones

Enterprise zones have been created in areas of industrial decay where it is hoped to attract businesses to regenerate the areas.

There are two major tax incentives available within the first ten years of a site being included in an enterprise zone.

- 100% first year capital allowances for both industrial and commercial buildings
- exemption from development land tax.

There are also other benefits to be gained from locating in these zones but beware that they are not swallowed up in higher rents or property prices:

- exemption from rates
- simplified planning procedures
- exemption from the need for industrial development certificates
- exemption from industrial training board requirements
- faster customs facilities
- minimal requests from government for statistical information.

The existing enterprise zones are within the following:

- Belfast
- Corby
- Dudley
- Glasgow
- Hartlepool
- Isle of Dogs
- Liverpool

- Manchester
- Newcastle/Gateshead
- Swansea
- Wakefield.

The following new enterprise zones have been announced:

- Allerdale
- Derbyshire (north-east)
- Kent (north-west)
- Lancashire (north-east)
- Middlesbrough
- Rotherham
- Scunthorpe
- Telford
- Wellingborough
- Tayside.

Could your expansion be in an enterprise zone?

Finance

Many expansion plans are frustrated by the non-availability or cost of finance. More will be said about this in Chapter 5 but remember that schemes exist to help you.

Three financial measures of investment worth

On what basis should a decision to make a capital investment be formed? The cost of the investment and the amount and timing of the expected cash benefits should be the cornerstones. Tax, government grants and finance are just some of the factors which you will have to examine to determine what are the real costs and benefits of your proposed investments.

How are we to make sense of the wealth of figures which this process creates?

Your research on each of your projects for capital investment should be brought together in a short report. One aspect of your appraisal will be the financial analysis but it should also include qualitative factors such as those mentioned at the beginning of the chapter.

Arguments rage in academic circles about how to measure investment worth in financial terms. In practice, the selection depends on circumstances. In other words, the selection itself is part of the judgment involved in the overall investment decision. The rest of the chapter looks at three different financial measures of investment worth in order to illustrate the principles. The choice of measure will be yours!

Consider the following project for investment in plant:

Initial cost at beginning of year 1	£12,000
Government selective assistance grant receivable after six months	£2,000
	£10,000
Estimated life in operation	4 years
Estimated disposal value	£2,000
The business pays tax at	50%
Capital allowances in year 1	100%

Tax is paid or recovered in the middle of the year following the relevant income or expense

Suppose that the net operating profits before depreciation in each year of the plant's useful life are:

Year 1   £2,000

Year 2   £4,000

Year 3   £5,000

Year 4   £5,000

Whichever method you use to appraise a project, first prepare a cash and profit forecast. Fig 4.2 shows the way of setting this out.

Here are our financial measures of investment worth for this project:

Payback.   This is simply the time which will elapse between making the initial expenditure and recovering it from the cash benefits expected from the project. In our example, this happens at the end of the second year, so the payback is 24 months.

To see this, look at the cash flow forecast in Fig 4.2. You will see that the cash break-even occurs at the end of year 2.

Another project with a payback of 20 months would be regarded as superior on this basis.

Fig 4.2   Cash and profit forecast

	Year 1 £	Year 2 £	Year 3 £	Year 4 £	Year 5 £	Total £
Capital cost						
Original outlay	(12,000)	—	—	—	—	(12,000)
Government grant	2,000	—	—	—	—	2,000
Disposal proceeds	—	—	—	2,000	—	2,000
Net capital cost (A)	(10,000)	—	—	2,000	—	(8,000)
Operating results						
Operating profit (B)	2,000	4,000	5,000	5,000	—	16,000
Depreciation	(2,000)	(2,000)	(2,000)	(2,000)	—	(8,000)
Loss on disposal	—	—	—	—	—	—
Net profit before tax	—	2,000	3,000	3,000	—	8,000
Cash flows						
Capital cost (A)	(10,000)	—	—	2,000	—	(8,000)
Operating profit (B)	2,000	4,000	5,000	5,000	—	16,000
Tax paid on operating profit	—	(1,000)	(2,000)	(2,500)	(2,500)	(8,000)
Tax relief on cost/ (balancing charge)	—	5,000	—	—	(1,000)	4,000
After-tax cash	(8,000)	8,000	3,000	4,500	(3,500)	4,000
Cumulative	(8,000)	—	3,000	7,500	4,000	

The method has the great advantage of simplicity. It also tends to give weight to projects which earn income sooner rather than later. The disadvantages are that it ignores proceeds received after the payback date and the timing of proceeds before then. Nevertheless, if cash is in short supply, this may be the most practical measure for you.

Fig 4.3   Balance sheet values

Year	Beginning of year	End of year	Average
	£	£	£
1	10,000	8,000	9,000
2	8,000	6,000	7,000
3	6,000	4,000	5,000
4	4,000	2,000	3,000
			24,000
			÷ 4
			£6,000

Accounting rate of return.   This is obtained by comparing the average pre-tax accounting profit with the average balance sheet value. In Fig 4.2, the average net profit before tax over the four years is £8,000/4, i.e. £2,000. The average balance sheet value is £6,000 as computed in Fig 4.3 above. Thus the accounting rate of return in this case is 2,000/6,000 x 100, i.e. 33%.

The method can be misleading.

The return of 33% appears high in relation to usual interest rates but the comparison is not valid since the method does not take into account the timing of the proceeds from the investment.

Net present value.   The concept is simple. Cash in hand today is worth more than cash tomorrow. The higher interest rates become, the greater the discrepancy. Set out in Fig 4.4 is a comparison of the cash flows from our project with their present values when interest is at 10% and 25%.

The net present value can be regarded as an unrealised capital gain from the investment over and above the minimum return required on the company's capital. If the minimum return required is 10%, the investment in our example is worthwhile because the present value is £1,976. At 25%, the project is not worthwhile, with a negative present value of £(365).

The return required is of course a planning decision (see Chapter 1) but will not be less than the return you could obtain on a safe external investment. The method is sometimes accused of being too difficult. Certainly the arithmetic is tedious. This is easily overcome with a calculator with a discounting function. The advantages of this method outweigh the £50 for the calculator.

Fig 4.4   Present value of cash flows

Year	Description	Cash flow £	Present value @ 10% £	Present value @ 25% £
1	Initial outlay	(12,000)	(12,000)	(12,000)
	Government grant	2,000	1,905	1,778
	Net operating receipts	2,000	1,905	1,778
2	Tax benefit of capital allowances	5,000	4,329	3,556
	Net operating receipts	3,000	2,597	2,133
3	Net operating receipts	3,000	2,361	1,707
4	Net operating receipts	2,500	1,789	1,138
	Disposal proceeds	2,000	1,366	819
5	Tax paid re year 4	(2,500)	(1,626)	(910)
	Tax charge on disposal proceeds	(1,000)	(650)	(364)
		4,000	1,976	(365)

Explanation.   Cash in hand today is worth more than cash in hand tomorrow. How much more? The answer depends on the return the company requires. Two examples of present value calculations are set out below.

The present value can be calculated simply by dividing the actual value by (100 + the rate of annual interest used) multiplied by 100 (i.e. moving the decimal point two places to the right) for *each* year. For a part year, divide by (100 + the appropriate proportion of the rate of annual interest used) and again move the decimal point two places.

Example A

Calculate the present value @ 10% interest of a Government grant of £2,000 received six months later.

$$\frac{£2,000}{(100 + (0.5 \times 10))} \times 100 = \frac{£2,000}{105} \times 100 = \underline{£1,905}$$

Example B

Calculate the present value @ 25% interest of net operating receipts of £3,000 received for Year 3 (= average of 2.5 years after start).

Year 1 $\frac{3,000}{125} \times 100 = \underline{£2,400}$

Year 2 $\frac{2,400}{125} \times 100 = \underline{£1,920}$

Year 3 $\frac{1,920}{112.5} \times 100 = \underline{£1,707}$

Fig 4.4   Present value of cash flows continued

Proof	Example A @ 10%	Example B @ 25%
Discounted sum	£1,905	£1,707
Interest 1st half-year	95	213
Original sum	£2,000	£1,920
Interest 2nd year		480
		£2,400
Interest 3rd year		600
Original sum		£3,000

A capital investment appraisal and government incentives checklist

1. Establish a formal procedure for appraising investment proposals including the costs and the benefits.   ☐

2. Ensure that you take advantage of government investment incentives including:

    ● tax reliefs   ☐

    ● grants   ☐

    ● enterprise zones   ☐

    ● finance   ☐

    and ensure that these are taken into account before the investment decision is made. If in doubt, consult an expert.   ☐

3. Select a method of measuring investment worth in financial terms which is appropriate for your business. If this is not the net present value method then be sure to identify precisely why not.   ☐

4. Investment is just one strategy for expansion and should be appraised in the context of your overall business planning.   ☐

Further action to be taken by me

1.

2.

3.

4.

5.

6.

Where to go for further help

Organisations

Equipment Leasing Association
18 Upper Grosvenor St., London W1X 9PB
Tel: 01-491 2783

National Enterprise Board
101 Newington Causeway, London SE1 6EU
Tel: 01-403 6666

Regional Development Grants Office, Department of Industry
Room 431, Kingsgate House, 66-74 Victoria St., London SW1E 6SJ
Tel: 01-212 6712

Books

Business Finance, B Ogley, Longman (1982): Ch 11

Capital Allowances in Law and Practice, R J Pickerill, ICAEW (1981)

Finance Leasing: A Guide for the Lessee in the UK, G Hubbard, The Institute of Cost and Management Accountants (1980)

Financial Management and Policy, J Van Horne, Prentice-Hall International (5th ed)

Industrial Aids in Britain, 1982: A Businessman's Guide, G Walker and K Allen, Centre for the Study of Public Policy, University of Strathclyde

Official Sources of Finance and Aid for Industry in the UK, 1982, National Westminster Bank

The Evaluation of Risk in Business Investment, J C Hall, Pergamon (1980)

The Lease Versus Buy Decision, H Bierman, Prentice-Hall International (1982)

Equipment Leasing, Equipment Leasing Association

5. RAISING FINANCE

Expansion needs financing. Few businesses will be able to do this from existing resources, so new money is usually needed. How should this money be raised? There is no simple answer, but there are some general guidelines.

Planning. It is comparatively easy to raise funds in advance of the need to spend, but almost impossible if the money is required to meet liabilities that are already due. Cash requirements must be planned (see Chapter 3).

Borrowings and shareholders' funds. What is the appropriate proportion of shareholders' funds to external borrowings? The answer depends very much on the terms of the borrowing, the profit growth the business is achieving and the nature of its assets. Most bankers are content with a 1:1 ratio of shareholders' funds to borrowings. If this ratio is to be exceeded it will almost always be necessary to put a special case to support the position to the lender. Remember also that interest payments depend on the size of the loan outstanding and not on profitability. The higher the proportion of borrowings to shareholders' funds the greater will be the impact of interest payments on the stability.

Matching assets and liabilities. It is important to match the terms of the various types of borrowing with the cash flow anticipated from the investment. For example, it is rarely wise to borrow short-term funds to build premises which will be used in the business for twenty years or more unless the cash flow indicates that it is possible.

There are many different sources of new finance. Having decided your financing strategy, don't hesitate to shop around for the best terms.

Risk capital

One primary source of risk capital will be from the existing proprietors. If a new business is formed, it is important to ensure from the beginning that the business is adequately capitalised. As the business expands it may be that the retained profits are sufficient to maintain a sound financial base. If there is rapid expansion, then the need for new capital may develop. Perhaps the existing proprietors have the resources to inject new funds and thus retain control. In a company this can be done by a rights issue. If, however, your expansion needs a considerable amount of new finance then outside investors must be found.

If you are a sole trader or a partnership, raising risk capital can be difficult. Existing proprietors are frequently hesitant to admit partners purely on their ability to finance the business. Investors frequently do not want the responsibility that partnership entails.

One of the advantages of corporate structure is the comparative ease with which risk capital can be raised. There are a number of ways of doing this:

Placing shares.   Some wealthy individuals are anxious to invest in venture capital. Institutions are constantly on the look out for opportunities for a high return. Both these groups provide a useful source of further capital. Consult your bank manager, merchant banker or stockbroker to see if shares can be placed through them.

Unlisted securities market(USM).   The USM provides a public market for shares. Entry to the market is much cheaper than obtaining a full listing on The Stock Exchange, mainly because of lower advertising costs. If you are prepared to relinquish some of your share capital and the market value of your business is between £1 million and £20 million then the USM is a good source of new capital.

This source of capital has other advantages. It may become practicable to acquire other companies using new shares as the purchase consideration rather than cash. It will also become possible for shareholders to dispose of part of their holdings to raise cash for their own needs more readily.

The USM is a comparatively new market. In the 1960s growing companies set their sights on 'going public'. It seems likely that in the 1980s 'going to the USM' will be a more familiar cry.

Bank overdrafts

The first source of external finance for most businesses is the bank. If a company's balance sheet is strong it may be possible to borrow without security. In most cases, however, the bank will seek a fixed charge over specified assets or possibly a floating charge over all the assets of the business. It is important to avoid providing too much security because this reduces flexibility in negotiating new borrowings. Try to limit charges to specific assets and avoid giving either group or personal guarantees.

The level of bank borrowing will normally grow as your business expands. It is important to control this growth and to maintain close relations with your bank manager. The vital steps are:

● always stay within your agreed bank overdraft limits

● provide your bank manager with accounts on a timely basis

● prepare forecasts that you expect to achieve when you are seeking additional facilities – over-optimistic forecasts which are not met will not impress your bank manager.

Remember that the most important thing is to develop a good relationship with your bank manager. This does not mean that you should not keep him on his toes by making sure that you know what his competition can offer.

Medium-term bank finance

An important form of finance for some expanding companies is a three to five-year loan from a clearing bank. These loans are not repayable on demand but by reference to a pre-determined timetable over the period of the loan. This can be particularly suitable to finance the purchase of plant or machinery or possibly the acquisition of a new subsidiary. This is a good example of matching the repayment of capital with the expected flow of cash from an investment.

Acceptance credits

Most companies only seek short-term finance from their clearing banker. It may be helpful in negotiating overdraft limits and interest rates if your banker is aware that there is competition. An ideal opportunity arises if you have a short-term requirement for funds to meet a temporary increase in current assets, to meet a large export order for example. In these circumstances you can go to a merchant bank who will arrange for a bill to be drawn which is guaranteed unconditionally by the bank. The bill can then be sold in the market at a discount which reflects current interest rates. On maturity the bank meets the bill and you repay the bank with the proceeds of the export order. This may prove cheaper than a bank overdraft but is only suitable for short-term finance in excess of £25,000.

Leasing and hire-purchase

When fixed assets are to be acquired, leasing or hire-purchase should always be considered. The difference between the two transactions is that at the end of the period of a hire-purchase agreement legal title passes to the hirer but in a pure lease this is not necessarily the case. Taxation generally plays an important part in assessing the advantages or disadvantages of these forms of finance and each situation needs to be considered individually. Broadly, the tax allowances are given to the hirer in the case of hire-purchase but to the lessor in the case of a lease.

Financial institutions

Such institutions are often prepared to lend a company money to finance expansion. They will often take risks but there is a price to pay. The price will generally involve giving the institution a right to equity participation. This may be either immediately or later through options or convertible preference shares. Granting such an interest may be helpful to a businessman because he has effectively gained a powerful new business partner who will be keen to increase the value of his stake and will be available for help and advice. On the other hand it does give away some independence and flexibility.

A raising finance checklist

1. Do your planning to identify the need for finance well in advance. ☐

2. Decide for your business what ratio of external borrowings to shareholders' funds is appropriate and do not exceed it. ☐

3. Match the terms of repayment of borrowings to the cash flow anticipated from each investment. ☐

4. Maintain close personal contact with your bank manager, both to keep him informed and on his toes. ☐

5. Review the security you have granted to ensure that it is the minimum consistent with your borrowing needs. ☐

6. Investigate the short-term fluctuations in your business to see if acceptance credits could be a useful form of finance. ☐

7. Always consider leasing or hire-purchase as an alternative to outright purchase of fixed assets. ☐

8. Consider financial institutions to help finance your expansion and view them as potential partners in the future of the business. ☐

Further action to be taken by me

1.

2.

3.

4.

5.

Where to go for further help

Organisations.   The best people to contact are your accountant and your bank manager.

Books

Business Finance, B Ogley, Longman (1981)

Company Administration Handbook, Gower (5th ed, 1982): Ch 6 Sources of finance, S Badger

Financial Management and Policy, J Van Horne, Prentice-Hall International (5th ed)

Financial Management Handbook, J E Broyles and I A Cooper, Gower (2nd ed, 1981)

Finding Money for Your Business, Confederation of British Industry (1982)

Management of Company Finance, Samuels and Wilkes, Van Nostrand Reinhold (3rd ed, previously published by Nelson)

Money for Business, Bank of England and City Communications Centre (1981)

The Management of Business Finance, J Freear, Pitman (1980)

6. ACQUISITIONS

Many businesses seek to expand by buying other businesses. This may seem to be an easy path to growth but the purchaser must beware. Most bankers, merchant bankers, accountants and others involved in finance have a long list of clients seeking good acquisition opportunities. The right opportunities however are difficult to find. If you wish to expand in this way, study your customers, competitors and suppliers and try to find your candidate before an auction develops.

When planning your acquisition a number of questions should be answered·

Why should you buy a business?

You should ideally have answered this question through your overall business planning and not as a 'spur of the moment' decision. Your plan should have identified in general terms the nature of the business you are looking for, including its products, markets, people, know-how, financial structure and the price you are prepared to pay. You are then in a position to actively look for what you want. In practice, opportunities often present themselves suddenly and the forethought and research that you have done will prove invaluable. If you have not planned an acquisition but a tempting opportunity presents itself, proceed with particular caution.

Who is going to run the business?

When an acquisition is planned, it is essential that you identify who is to run the new business. In some cases, it is clear that the existing management is sound and are prepared to stay on. In this case a major feature of the negotiations should be to agree their terms of employment. It is important to ensure that the management team not only agree to remain but also have the incentive to continue the business successfully.

Alternatively, you may have identified a different management team with the necessary skills and experience to run the new business. In this case, a key feature of the purchase negotiations will be to agree the terms under which the existing management will leave.

Remember that it is almost always a mistake to acquire a business without first identifying an effective management team to run it. Such an acquisition is like a rudderless ship and only good luck will prevent a major loss.

What are you buying?

If a business has the strength of a solid asset base and a record of growing profits it is probably not for sale. You are more likely to find a business which has shown significant growth but which is hungry for cash. In this case, you must assess the capital requirements before deciding to buy. Beware of the business which has reached its peak of profitability and is for sale because the vendor believes that future trends are downwards. If profits are vital to you, ensure that the past profits record can be maintained.

If a business for sale has a dull profit record, then the assets are likely to be your central concern. Make sure that those assets really exist and that you will acquire proper title to them. Insist on an independent valuation and perhaps obtain an independently audited balance sheet at the completion date. Do not forget to check that fixed assets are properly maintained. Most important of all, check that there are no unrecorded liabilities. Unfunded pensions liabilities are an important and common example.

How much should you pay?

There is no simple answer to this. Techniques of capital investment appraisal (see Chapter 4) will help but, in the end, it comes down to what you are prepared to offer and the vendor to accept. In principle, if a business is failing to achieve an adequate return on capital employed, you should expect to acquire it for something less than the book value of the assets. If profits are growing satisfactorily, it is probable that a premium over book value will have to be paid.

How should you pay?

The purchase and sale agreement is an extremely important element of a successful acquisition. One important aspect of this is the nature of the consideration which must be tailored to the circumstances.

If, for example, the owner is selling his entire interest and is playing no further part in its operation he will probably want to sell for cash. The agreement may contain guarantees and warranties but once he has the money it is difficult to recover any part of your investment if it goes wrong. This is the sort of occasion where the steps described earlier to verify assets and liabilities would have paid off.

Another example would be the business with high expectation of growth in earnings, low net assets and continued involvement in management by the vendor. In this case it might be appropriate to defer a substantial part of the consideration and make it dependent on the achievement of future earnings. This has the disadvantage that the vendor would normally expect a premium on this basis but at least most of the consideration is only paid if the earnings growth continues.

If you have a company with marketable shares, then you may be able to offer these as consideration and avoid paying cash. This is an important advantage of joining the Unlisted Securities Market or obtaining a quote on The Stock Exchange.

Will rationalisation lead to savings?

A common expectation of an acquisition is achieving economies through rationalisation of the two businesses. Unfortunately this often does not work as planned, at least in the short term. There are many reasons for this including, for example:

- the cost of redundancy
- the tendency for employee benefits to settle at the highest of the levels offered by each business separately
- the dislocation and cost caused by moving premises and the difficulty of selling specialist buildings
- the difficulty of standardising long established systems designed for different products etc..

These can, of course, be overcome with goodwill on both sides but it is unwise to rely on economies of scale as the main reason for an acquisition.

What are the tax considerations?

As a purchaser, your tax considerations will differ from those of the vendor.

Where a company carries on the business you are acquiring, the vendor will usually want to sell the shares in the company rather than the assets themselves. In this way, the vendor will normally restrict his tax liability to capital gains tax on the sale proceeds. Moreover, a sale of shares will mean that the cash is received directly by the individual vendor and is not locked in the company.

A sale of the assets of the company as opposed to a sale of shares is likely to create additional tax liabilities. Such sales may give rise to the clawback of tax depreciation allowances in the company and will almost certainly do so in the case of plant and machinery. Capital gains liabilities may arise on the sale of certain assets such as property and goodwill. In addition, the vendor has the problem of extracting cash from the company which will place further tax liabilities on him individually.

On the other hand, as a purchaser, you will probably wish to acquire the assets of the business rather than the shares of the company which carries it on. There are two main reasons for this. First, you can then obtain capital allowances on plant and machinery based on the purchase price. On a share purchase, the allowances on plant and machinery will be restricted to the unrelieved expenditure, if any, of the company itself. You may also obtain some industrial buildings allowances.

However, on an assets purchase, there are likely to be differences of opinion between the vendor and the purchaser over the allocation of the total price between the assets. The purchaser will want the consideration to be allocated to assets which give him maximum tax relief, e.g. plant or stock. The vendor will not want the consideration to be so weighted as this is likely to involve him in heavier tax charges. He will look to the price being allocated, so far as possible, towards assets where any profit will be treated as a capital gain. Nevertheless, the potential area of conflict may not be so important where the company which is selling the assets has tax losses which can be used to cover any income profits on their disposal.

Second, the acquisition of a company means that the purchaser acquires not only the shares of that company but also all the liabilities of and potential future claims against the company arising out of past events. There may be, for example, commercial and tax liabilities which are undiscovered as yet. The protection to be obtained by warranties and indemnities may not be an entirely comprehensive insurance. On any acquisition of a company, it is very desirable that a full investigation is made into potential liabilities.

Although a purchaser may wish to acquire assets, your views could be changed if the company has tax losses. Such losses may be used to cover future trading profits of the company.

Also, to overcome the problem of the possible contingent liabilities mentioned earlier, or to meet the case where the purchase involves only part of the company's total business, the trade, or the part concerned, can be transferred to a new company and the shares in that new company sold to the purchasers. In these circumstances, the trading losses relating to the trade are still available to be carried forward. Whichever method is adopted, there are a number of areas which have to be watched carefully. Unused trading losses can only be carried forward against profits of the same trade. It is therefore necessary to make sure that the carry forward of losses cannot be denied on the grounds that the company is not carrying on the same trade.

A further anti-avoidance provision may prevent the use of brought-forward losses even though the same trade is carried on. The legislation denies such use if there is both a change in the ownership of a company and a major change in the nature or conduct of the trade within a period of three years before or after the ownership change. Such a change includes a major change in the type of property dealt in, or services provided, or a major change in customers, outlets or markets of the trade.

There is similar legislation dealing with the carry forward of unused advance corporation tax. You may wish to make substantial changes to the business and, therefore, the potential application of this legislation has to be carefully monitored.

There are two further points to watch on the acquisition of the shares of a company. Certain capital gains charges may arise in the company being acquired immediately on the transfer of the shares. This can occur where the company has acquired assets from a group company within the preceding six years. A charge to development land tax can arise similarly on land acquired intra-group within the same period.

Whether the outcome is the purchase of the assets of, or of shares in, the company, it is usually possible to reach agreement on the sale consideration. It may, however, be necessary for adjustments to be made to the price because the particular method adopted results in substantial tax advantages to one party to the detriment of the other. It may also be necessary to provide for the price to be varied dependent on the final availability of tax losses.

Making a decision

The appraisal of a potential acquisition will ultimately depend on your judgment. The judgment can be supported by evidence, such as independently verified valuations and audited accounts but qualitative factors also play their part. Paramount among the qualitative factors is your assessment of the management but all sorts of other factors also count. These include the people, the marketing approach, compatibility of products, working practices and a host of others. The message is 'look before you leap'.

An acquisitions checklist

1. Identify your acquisition target carefully by a thorough study of your customers, competitors and suppliers. Your professional advisors may also be able to help. ☐

2. Do your homework on the business to be acquired thoroughly and gather details of:

   ● the history and legal structure ☐

   ● existing proprietors ☐

   ● existing management ☐

   ● premises and plant, including their value and any outstanding commitments ☐

   ● products and methods of manufacture ☐

   ● sales and marketing including pricing policy, major customers and distribution ☐

   ● major suppliers ☐

   ● the management reporting system and controls ☐

   ● past financial results ☐

   ● taxation ☐

   ● future prospects. ☐

3. Be absolutely sure that you are satisfied that you have an effective management team available to run the business. ☐

4. Establish in your own mind whether you are buying assets or profits. ☐

5. Negotiate the price but don't forget to apply techniques of capital investment appraisal (see Chapter 4). ☐

6. Tailor the purchase consideration to suit the circumstances and reduce the risk of a major cash loss. ☐

7. Avoid relying too heavily on realising economies of scale through acquisition. ☐

8. Consult an expert on the tax considerations. ☐

9. Consult a lawyer on the form of the acquisition agreement, in particular the inclusion of warranties. ☐

10. Don't forget the qualitative factors when reaching a final decision. ☐

Further action to be taken by me

1.

2.

3.

4.

5.

6.

Where to go for further help

Organisations

It is likely that all your professional advisors will need to be involved but, in the first instance, contact your accountant.

Books

Acquisition and Corporate Development, J W Bradley and D H Horn, Lexington (1980)

Acquisitions and Mergers, J G Williams, ICAEW (1980)

Acquisitions of Private Companies, W L Knight, Oyez (1982)

Business Finance, B Ogley, Longman (1981): Ch 17

Company Administration Handbook, Gower (5th ed, 1982): Ch 9 Managing Merger and Acquisitions, L H Verreck

Company Finance, Takeovers and Mergers: Essential Business Law, G Morse, Sweet and Maxwell (1979)

7. SELLING MORE

Selling more of your products or services is likely to be central to your expansion plans. There is no simple formula for doing this but one of the most important first steps is to define your products and identify their markets.

Can you say what it is that makes your products unique? What are the characteristics of your customers? Answering these seemingly obvious questions have led many businesses to change direction. One example was a teacher who established a language school for foreigners. He believed that his customers were serious students of language and he therefore provided a high standard of teaching but in a rather depressing environment. He was extremely surprised when he discovered that most of his customers joined his courses hoping for an enjoyable holiday in England. The teacher had by now become a businessman and he put more emphasis on comfort and social activities, thereby reducing his costs. He soon had more applicants than he could accommodate and was able to put his prices up.

Knowing what your products are and the characteristics of your customers is not enough. Are you sure that your marketing methods are those best suited to the circumstances? For example, packaging is of prime importance for selling perfume but irrelevant to a machine tool. In our example of the language school, the advertising approach, including the design of the school's brochures, had to be changed to reflect a holiday spirit rather than serious study.

Remember that marketing is a subject in its own right and you should ask yourself whether your business has the level of skill needed. You can of course read books or attend training courses but sooner or later you should consider taking expert advice.

Selling to the same customers

Are there opportunities to sell more of your existing products to your existing customers? Analyse the products sold to each customer and the frequency of his orders in relation to his size and business to ensure that he is buying across your complete range and that he is buying the major proportion of his supplies from you.

Remember that a buyer will take many factors into account when making a purchasing decision, not just price. Identify what it is that differentiates your product from the competition and build on that. This may be quality, delivery performance, after-sales service, the provision of advertising to help a retailer sell your product, etc. Beware of believing that price alone will sell your product.

There may be ways to make your products more attractive by special offers or free gifts. This is quite common in consumer markets but can be used more generally. In our example of the language school, new business was obtained from overseas companies by offering free flights to the UK for their managers if they attended language courses in the UK during the summer. This appealed to those managers who were going to England at that time anyway.

There may also be ways to help your customers increase their sales and thereby purchases from you. If, for example, you sell to retailers, consider running a promotional campaign funded jointly by yourself and them. The campaign might include local advertising, specific price reductions for a period, 'two for the price of one' offers or 'give-aways'.

New markets for the same products

If your share of the total market for your type of products is small then there are almost certainly opportunities to sell more. You should start by identifying who your potential new customers are.

First find out who your competitors' customers are. They will often be potential customers for you. Try scanning the trade magazines and the entries in Yellow Pages which are under the same headings as your own customers. It is also possible to buy lists of names. The usefulness of this technique will depend on how accurate your definition of your potential customer is and you will often be paying for useless names. Nevertheless, as computer records become more sophisticated, so the market intelligence has become more effective. Almost all middle income groups now receive direct mail approaches once or twice a week. The success rate on this method is often much less than one per cent but this can be cost-effective nevertheless.

Identifying new markets depends on your knowledge of the exact nature of the product you are selling and its uses. This may lead you to identify new customers who will use the product in the same way, or new uses of the product in completely different industries or processes. For example, a food product normally sold direct to the public through retailers may, with some minor modifications to its packaging, be saleable to the catering trade for direct use.

Another way of opening up the market for your products is to establish a franchising operation.

New products

Ideas for new products can come from many sources:

- Your sales-force may identify products that complement your existing range which it could sell to existing customers

- Flashes of inspiration can come from your employees. A suggestions box with a small reward for accepted ideas can be a good idea

- Specific market research

● A customer with a particular need may suggest that you design a product in conjunction with him. This can be very attractive because it makes it very difficult for your competitors to offer an equivalent alternative. Beware, however, of spending a lot of time and money developing a new product which will have only a limited market. It is of little value, for example, designing a cog for one of your customers who has three machines in which it fits. Total sales volume is unlikely to exceed four, and that includes a spare!

The important thing is that you remain open-minded to new ideas from whichever source they come.

Once you have an idea, estimate the cost of production and the price at which you think it would sell. Then do some market research to determine how many you might be able to sell. You do not have to use an external market research organisation. A well planned exercise carried out by your own staff and using existing contacts may suffice. Do not fool yourself by being over-optimistic and ensure that you will be able to generate repeat sales in the future. Decide how the new product would be sold. For example, would it need a heavy advertising budget, are your current salesmen technically competent to sell it effectively, will you have to offer an in-stock service, etc.?

If the idea looks like a winner and your forecasts indicate that you can make and sell it at a profit, prepare your detailed budgets for a trial period. Be ruthless in reviewing your performance against the budget and do not hesitate to axe the new product if it does not match up to expectations. There is little worse than pouring more and more time, money and effort into a 'dud' product, often at considerable cost to your mainstream business. If you do have to drop a product do not be depressed. However well planned and researched new ideas are, some just do not take off. Return to the drawing-board and start again!

Another idea is to complement your existing range by becoming an agent for an overseas manufacturer. This has the advantage of increasing your sales without requiring a corresponding investment in manufacturing capacity. Beware, however, of becoming too dependent upon such sales. If you lose the agency for any reason you could suddenly find yourself with a large sales-force and an expensive administrative structure with no sales to support them.

The sales-force

The performance of your sales-force is likely to be vital to your drive for increased sales. The salesmen need to be closely monitored and controlled to ensure that they are generating additional profitable sales and not just additional sales.

Ensure that they are well briefed on new products, including their strengths and weaknesses and the new markets that you want to attack.

Set realistic targets that you expect each salesman to achieve. Be careful not to forget about the existing business, however: the established customers must not be ignored in the enthusiasm to acquire new ones.

Incentive schemes for salesmen can work if they are well designed. Additional sales are no good if the customer does not, for example, pay for the goods within the established credit period. So consider including a penalty factor within the scheme to discourage sales which become bad debts. Beware also of allowing your salesmen too much flexibility for offering discounts. It is always very hard to increase the price next time. Marginal costing is fine for marginal decisions but it is the best road to bankruptcy if it is applied to all pricing decisions.

Advertising

There is an expression which says 'half of all promotional expenditure is wasted, the problem is identifying which half'! Try to analyse the results of your previous promotional efforts to determine 'which half'. This is not easy because the impact of stopping an advertising campaign often does not show up until some time later. Some perseverance in this area, however, will often be well rewarded.

Before starting a campaign, decide precisely who the target audience is and design the campaign accordingly. For example, a toy-maker may believe that the motivation to buy his toys comes primarily from the children and not the parents, so there is little point in advertising in the local evening paper which children very rarely read.

A selling more checklist

1. For each of your products define in writing precisely:

    ● what market you are in ☐

    ● what they are ☐

    ● what their existing uses are ☐

    ● all the alternative uses ☐

    ● the unique selling points ☐

    ● who buys them ☐

    ● who else might buy them ☐

    ● the size of each of your markets and your position within it. ☐

2. Review your skills in marketing and consider:

    ● training ☐

    ● taking expert advice. ☐

3. Review your marketing methods to ensure that they are compatible with your product definition and target customers. Include in your review:

- pricing ☐
- packaging ☐
- advertising ☐
- promotion ☐
- distribution methods ☐
- use of sales-force ☐
- brochures and other literature ☐
- market research. ☐

4. Review your existing customers and identify opportunities for selling them more. ☐

5. Establish a target list of potential new customers. ☐

6. Review your procedures for generating new ideas to ensure that your business remains responsive and creative. ☐

7. Research new products and their markets in depth before launching them and prepare detailed targets for them in the usual way. ☐

8. Be ruthless in axeing 'dud' products. ☐

9. Keep your salesmen thoroughly briefed and monitor their performance closely. ☐

Further action to be taken by me

1.

2.

3.

4.

5.

6.

Where to go for further help

Organisations

Institute of Marketing
Moor Hall, Cookham, Maidenhead, Berkshire SL6 9QH
Tel: 062 85 24922

Statistics and Market Intelligence Library
Export House, 50 Ludgate Hill, London EC4M 7HU
Tel: 01-248 5757

Books

Effective Marketing Management, C Kennedy and M Willis, Gower (1981, previously Introduction to Marketing – The Cranfield Approach, published by MCB Books)

Fundamentals and Practice of Marketing, J Wilmshurst, Heinemann/ Institute of Marketing (1978)

Fundamentals of Modern Marketing, E W Cundiff and R R Still, Prentice-Hall International (3rd ed)

Introducing Marketing, M Christopher, G Wills and M McDonald, Pan Books (1981)

Marketing, G B Giles, Macdonald and Evans (1978)

Marketing – An Introduction, M J Baker, Macmillan (3rd ed, 1971)

Marketing Management-Analysis, Planning and Control, P Kotler, Prentice-Hall International (4th ed, 1980)

Principles of Marketing, P Kotler, Prentice-Hall International (1980)

The Basic Arts of Marketing, R Willsmer, Business Books (1976)

The Management of Marketing, Wilson, Gower (1981)

8. DOING BUSINESS ABROAD

One way to expand is to attack new markets. There are many businesses which have rejected selling overseas, believing that exporting is too difficult.

Certainly there are difficulties, but identifying them and planning how to tackle them is half the battle. Do your homework carefully by establishing where your potential markets are. You can begin by using the Export Intelligence Division of the British Overseas Trade Board. This is the main export promotion branch of the Department of Trade. Concentrate on particular areas or countries and do not try to spread your efforts too widely. Your review of each country should include an overview of:

- national characteristics
- economic trends
- business practices
- politics
- law
- taxation
- banking facilities
- exchange controls
- import controls.

The British Overseas Trade Board publishes booklets on most countries. Among its other services, it may contribute towards the costs of market research. The Export Credits Guarantee Department (ECGD) should be able to provide information to help you assess the risks.

How to sell?

Having determined the potential overseas markets for your products, the next question is how to sell?

In Europe and North America the best approach is often direct-selling using your own salesmen. Of prime importance is your ability to provide after-sales service, prompt delivery and a local stockholding.

Elsewhere, it is essential to have an agent, particularly for the Middle East, Africa, the Far East and South America. It is common for groups of companies selling a complementary range of products to form consortia and achieve a greater degree of success and efficiency selling together through one salesman or agent than they would selling individually.

The right selection of overseas salesmen and agents obviously is vital.

61

They must have the usual technical knowledge and selling ability and also have a thorough knowledge of the countries involved and speak the language. The last point is often overlooked by the British!

When selecting agents, you can use British Embassies or High Commissions to provide lists of possibilities and their credit ratings, etc. You should look for an agent who is in your line of business but is not selling competitors' products.

Having determined which of your products have export potential, where that potential is, and how you are going to realise it, you will need to set up a control system. This will involve agreeing budgets and targets for your agents and chasing them hard, if the targets are not achieved. Remember that you can nearly always change your agent if he fails to perform. On a cautionary note, you should check the local law on the appointment of agents first. The Embassy or High Commission should be able to help.

The agent's remuneration will generally be in the form of a retainer and a commission on sales made. Do not be afraid to haggle over percentages! In return for the retainer, you should expect to receive general market and economic intelligence and specific advice concerning your products, prices charged, etc. Be sure to specify this in the original contract.

Having appointed an agent, do not expect him to perform well if you then ignore him. Make sure he is fully briefed on all product developments and aim to visit him and his major customers two or three times per year.

Finally, it is no good going to all the effort of selling overseas unless you get paid! Your bank can be of considerable assistance with the formalities. Some of the financial aspects which need to be considered follow.

Choice of currency

Marketing considerations. Some overseas importers may prefer to deal in their own currency. You then have to handle the complications that come from fluctuations in foreign exchange rates until the contract is complete. Other customers may wish to contract in sterling if they have pounds to spend, or because they feel that sterling is likely to appreciate against their own currency. Local exchange controls may also affect their views.

The only general rule is that the exporter should be willing to find out in which currency his customer wishes to pay and, provided that this is convertible, discuss with his bank how best to meet his customer's wishes.

Prudence. In most cases, the UK exporter's costs arise in sterling. If the contract is priced in foreign currency the most prudent course is to cover the exchange risk. You should discuss this with your bank. Do not attempt to become a currency speculator, however exciting some of the stories you hear at the golf club may sound.

Terms of business

Any business contract requires care, in order to avoid misunderstanding when the time for payment arrives. With overseas business, this is particularly relevant.

Make sure that you have a clear agreement on:

● responsibility for shipment and related costs

● the point at which title passes to the buyer

● insurance in transit

● terms of credit

● the method of payment

● the role of the agent in the shipping, billing and collection process

● commission payable to agents, particularly in the event of bad debts.

You should be particularly careful to choose the best method of payment. A fundamental decision is whether the agent will bill the customer and collect cash on your behalf, or whether to deal direct.

There is no simple right answer to this. Your choice will depend on your assessment of the integrity and efficiency of your agent, administrative convenience, local trading conditions, exchange control and above all the cash flow implications. Some agents are slower payers than their customers! Remember that until cash is convertible into sterling there is an exchange risk, even if the cash is held by your agent.

Settlement

The details of the actual payment also need thought. The international banking system offers a variety of forms of money transfer. For trusted customers, a telegraphic transfer may be the quickest and most satisfactory answer. If, however, there is:

● doubt as to the overseas customer's ability or willingness to pay promptly

● lack of information about the overseas customer's status

● shortage of hard currency in the country concerned,

then you would be wise to consider using irrevocable letters of credit (ILC). If you are in any doubt about the status of the bank issuing the ILC, you should have it confirmed. Your bank manager will explain the procedure.

63

The ECGD is prepared to cover sales to certain markets only against a confirmed ILC.

You should be satisfied that you have received a letter of credit which is acceptable in every respect before embarking upon any expense in relation to the preparation of the order for shipment. The validity of the credit should be restricted to the period required up to the shipment and subsequent presentation of documents. This avoids incurring unnecessary bank charges.

You should also ensure that the method of shipment and the documentation are clearly specified in the contract. A freight agent's advice on this subject may be helpful. Failure by the exporter to comply exactly with the requirements of the credit will lead to delay in payment, while the advising bank cables to the opening bank for instructions.

It is good practice for an exporter's invoices to give details concerning his bank account, including:

● bank's name

● branch address and sorting code

● account name and number.

For details of other forms of settlement, contact your bank manager.

Credit insurance

Do consider credit insurance, particularly for high risk business such as large contracts or contracts with unstable countries.

Some credit insurance cover on overseas sales is available from commercial sources, but the main source of cover is the ECGD. Although large transactions may be insured individually, the ECGD handles smaller transactions on a 'whole turnover' basis, under which the ECGD will cover the whole of the policy-holder's export business.

The policy-holder will be asked to:

● obtain from the ECGD a credit limit for each overseas customer

● provide monthly details of his overseas sales

● pay a small insurance premium.

Since it may take time to obtain credit limits, you should contact the ECGD at an early stage.

Although the ECGD does not lend money directly, it can help the exporter give credit to his overseas customer by providing a guarantee to the exporter's bank, thereby enabling that bank to re-finance him. The simplest method is the discount by the bank, at very fine rates, of 180-day bills drawn on the exporter's overseas customer. More complex schemes exist to provide overseas customers with finance for major items of capital plant, and for large projects, at fine interest rates.

Recording

If you are billing in foreign currency for the first time, your accounting system will require some modification. Your individual customers' accounts should be maintained in both sterling and the foreign currency. This will enable you to match remittances to the related invoices in currency and identify exchange profits and losses quite simply, as they arise. In your financial statements, the total of the customers' accounts should be translated at the exchange rate prevailing at the accounting date unless you have covered the risk by forward exchange contracts.

Remember that VAT is zero-rated on export sales.

A doing business abroad checklist

1. Research potential overseas markets with great care and gather information on each country including:

   - national characteristics ☐
   - economic trends ☐
   - business practices ☐
   - politics ☐
   - law ☐
   - taxation ☐
   - banking facilities ☐
   - exchange controls ☐
   - import controls. ☐

2. Evaluate the commitment you will have to give to:

   - after-sales service ☐
   - prompt delivery ☐
   - local stock holding. ☐

3. Select the method of selling which is appropriate to each country and appoint agents or salesmen accordingly. Agree a contract covering the services you will receive and the remuneration to be paid. ☐

4. Control the activities of salesmen and agents by involving them in setting sales targets and expenditure budgets and monitoring them rigorously. ☐

65

5. Establish a foreign currency policy and monitor exchange risks with great care. ☐

6. Establish clear terms of business with overseas customers particularly in relation to terms of shipment and payment. ☐

7. Establish an efficient system for settlement of overseas transactions. ☐

8. Establish a credit control policy and consider exporters insurance. ☐

9. Ensure that your accounting system is modified to record overseas business efficiently. ☐

10. Your export drive will succeed if you do your homework first. ☐

Further action to be taken by me

1.

2.

3.

4.

5.

6.

Where to go for further help

Organisations

British Overseas Trade Board
1 Victoria St., London SW1H 0ET
Tel: 01-215 5773

British Standards Institution, Technical Help to Exporters
Maylands Ave., Hemel Hempstead, Herts. HP2 4SQ
Tel: 0442 3111

Export Credits Guarantee Department
Aldermanbury House, Aldermanbury Square, London EC2P 2EL
Tel: 01-606 6699

Institute of Export
World Trade Centre, Europe House, East Smithfield, London E1 9AA
Tel: 01-488 4766

International Chamber of Commerce, British Nationals Committee
Centrepoint, 103 New Oxford St., London WC1A 1QB
Tel: 01-240 5558

Books

British Exports and Exchange Restrictions Abroad, Swiss Bank Corporation (1981)

Business and the Language Barrier, R Simpkin and R Jones, Business Books (1976)

Corporate Currency Risk, J A Donaldson, Financial Times (1980)

Credit Management, R M V Bass, Business Books (1979): Part 2 Export Credit Management

Currency Management, R Lassen, Woodhead-Faulkner (1982)

Debt Collection Letters in Ten Languages, J Butterworth, Gower (1978)

Exchange Risk and Exposure, R M Levich and C G Wihlboog (editors), Lexington (1980)

Export Credit: The Effective and Profitable Management of Export Credit and Finance, H. Edwards, Gower (1982, previously published by Shaws Linton)

Finance of International Trade, A Watson, The Institute of Bankers (1981)

Finance of International Trade, D P Whiting, Macdonald and Evans (4th ed, 1981)

International Trade: Essential Business Law, F Rose, Sweet and Maxwell (1979)

Management of Foreign Exchange Risk, L L Jacque, Lexington (1978)

Schmitthoff's Export Trade: The Law and Practice of International Trade, C Schmitthoff, Stevens (1980)

Selling, Importing and Exporting, Managing Your Business Guides, Hamlyn (1980): Part 3 Exporting

The Elements of Export Practice, A E Branch, Chapman and Hall (1979)

9. OVERSEAS INVESTMENT

Expansion through overseas investment often follows a successful export drive. A more permanent overseas base may be needed because the business may have outgrown the capacity of the local agent. Sometimes, however, an investment is required before any business can be done. An example is the construction industry, where a local presence is almost certainly a prerequisite. Whichever route your business has taken, there are some basic questions to answer when doing your planning. Inevitably, international taxation plays an important part and you should consult specialists when answering these questions for your business. Do not let the technical considerations, however, outweigh your commercial judgment. For example, you must be satisfied with the quality of the local management.

How should the investment be structured?

The fundamental decision is whether the investment should be in a branch of the UK company or a separate subsidiary. The usual commercial considerations may dictate this, such as the need for local participation or limited liability. Taxation will also be a major factor.

One tax advantage of a branch structure is that initial losses may be set against UK profits. This happens because the results of an overseas branch are automatically included in the results of the UK company for UK tax purposes.

However, one disadvantage of a branch structure is that, in practice, it is more difficult to establish its taxable profits or losses than those of a separate subsidiary. For example, there are practical difficulties in charging an overseas branch with a proportion of head office costs. A management charge from a UK parent company to a subsidiary, however, is easier to establish, as long as it is properly documented. A similar point applies to interest charges. Some further tax points are made later.

The right answer will depend on your own circumstances but more often than not a separate subsidiary proves to be the best solution.

How should the investment be financed?

Budgets and cash flow projections for the overseas investment will indicate the amount of fixed and working capital needed. Working capital is normally best provided by a local bank, probably an overseas branch or an associate of your UK bankers. Fixed capital should normally be provided by you in the form of share capital or long-term loans. The precise capital ratios will be influenced by local rules and practices. In many countries, such as the United States, France and Canada, loans from the controlling shareholder are treated as share capital for tax purposes where the amount of loan finance is excessive in relation to the share capital. What is 'excessive' varies a great deal from country to country and from business to business. A ratio of 1:1 is usually acceptable but this is a matter on which local advice should be sought. There may also be requirements for local residents to take a percentage of the share capital. This is common in the Middle East and Far East, for example.

If funds are being borrowed by the UK business to make the investment, then, as a general rule, the currency of the borrowings should match the currency of the investment. This will help minimise the risk from exchange rate movements. Unfortunately, there are taxation complications to consider. For example, exchange losses on long-term borrowings are not normally deductible for UK tax purposes. It may, however, be possible to structure the transaction in such a way that some relief is obtained. Professional advice should be sought first. Exchange profits on long-term borrowings are not taxable but it would be unwise to plan on the basis that these will arise. By contrast, exchange profits on the realisation of the overseas investment will be liable to capital gains tax.

You should also consider the availability of tax relief for any interest paid on borrowings. In most cases, it would be appropriate to borrow funds from your UK bankers to ensure a tax deduction for interest paid against UK profits.

What happens to repatriated funds?

Before any overseas investment is made, you must ensure that capital and profits can be freely repatriated to the UK. If local exchange controls seriously inhibit repatriation, then you should consider abandoning the investment plan.

If you are investing in an overseas company, then repatriation of profits by dividends will normally give rise to tax liabilities one way or another. Many countries levy a withholding tax on dividends. Where the UK has a double taxation agreement with the country, the withholding tax rate is generally reduced to 15% or less. The dividends received are taxable in the UK as well. Fortunately, however, credit is given for any overseas withholding taxes paid. In addition, UK companies owning 10% or more of the share capital of an overseas subsidiary are given a credit for the overseas taxes paid on the profits out of which the dividends are made. This is known as credit for 'underlying tax'.

An example may help clarify this. Suppose a UK company investing in the US through a US subsidiary receives a dividend of £9,500 after withholding tax of £500. The profits of the subsidiary have suffered US taxes (both Federal and State) of 50%:

	£	£
Dividend received		9,500
Add: withholding tax		500
Dividend declared		10,000
US underlying taxes		10,000
Gross profit used to pay dividend		20,000
Corporation tax @ 52%		10,400
Less:		
withholding tax	500	
underlying tax	10,000	10,500
		(100)
UK corporation tax liability		NIL

In this example, the relief for both the US withholding and underlying tax exceeds the UK tax liabilities so no UK tax is due. Unfortunately the excess US tax cannot be recovered.

If your investment overseas is in a local branch and not a company, then it is likely that profits can be repatriated without any local withholding tax. Take care, however, because there are exceptions, such as Canada and France.

Residence

It is important for legal and tax reasons to establish the residence of your overseas operation. Most countries regard companies as resident where they are incorporated. Where the business is actually managed and controlled may be important too. Companies established overseas to conduct local business operations will therefore invariably be resident where they are incorporated.

For UK tax purposes, a company is resident where it is managed and controlled and the place of incorporation is irrelevant. Management and control has been regarded as the control exercised by directors at Board meetings and residence of a company is determined mainly on the basis of where the directors meet.

When your overseas company is formed, take care to avoid the company being resident both locally and in the UK. This means that all directors' meetings should be held outside the UK.

Tax havens

For many years, the use of tax havens to avoid paying tax has caught the imagination of businessmen. Generally, widespread avoidance is prevented because:

● overseas transactions may require the consent of the Treasury (see below)

● the Inland Revenue has powers to adjust prices charged on transactions between related business operations in different countries if these are not at normal arm's-length prices

● there is a risk that the income of overseas companies may be treated as the income of individual UK shareholders.

This is a highly technical and changing area and if you are in any doubt always consult an expert.

Treasury consent

Treasury consent is required for a number of overseas transactions, including the formation of an overseas subsidiary and for an overseas subsidiary to issue shares or debentures. The latter is widely interpreted to include any debts evidenced in writing.

Consent can be general or special. A general consent covers the formation of a first-tier subsidiary but special consent is required for the issue of debentures. As a general rule, consent is forthcoming for any commercial transaction, provided its objective is not the avoidance of UK tax.

Reporting and accounting

The need for financial discipline is just as important for your overseas operations as for any others.

Do not allow yourself to be persuaded that, due to different local customs, your carefully established management reporting systems do not apply. You will of course have to deal with fluctuating currencies but even this can often be kept simple:

● Local management are not responsible for fluctuations in the value of their country's currency. The monitoring of the effectiveness of their management should therefore normally be in local currency. The budget and the regular financial reporting package can be prepared in local currency.

● Your investment overseas will almost certainly be with long-term prospects in mind. The cost will originally have been measured in sterling. Naturally you will be interested in the value of your investment subsequently but it is not necessary to constantly adjust the book value unless the value of the underlying business falls below cost.

● Ensure that amounts owing to and from overseas operations are agreed regularly. This should normally be at least monthly.

● Periodically, at least annually, you should incorporate the results of your overseas operation into those of the UK operation. There are technical complications depending on how much of the overseas operation you own. In most cases the accounts can simply be translated into sterling at the exchange rate ruling at the date the accounts are made up to.

It is important that distance does not become the excuse for failing to monitor overseas investments. The cost of air fares is small compared with the risk of failure. The goodwill created by visits from the 'head office' is important, too.

An overseas investment checklist

1. Ensure that your initial planning covers:

   ● adequacy of local management ☐

   ● how the investment will be structured ☐

   ● how the investment will be financed ☐

   ● repatriation of funds ☐

   ● taxation. ☐

2. Establish sound budgeting and management reporting systems. ☐

3. Ensure that your accounting procedures are modified to record the investment and ensure that amounts owing to and from overseas operations are agreed regularly. ☐

4. Visit your overseas locations from time to time to create goodwill and monitor progress. ☐

Further action to be taken by me

1.

2.

3.

4.

5.

6.

Where to go for further help

Organisation

British Overseas Trade Board
1 Victoria St., London SW1H 0ET
Tel: 01-215 5773

Books

Assessing Foreign Subsidiary Performance – Systems and Practices of Leading Multinational Companies, Business International Corporation (1982)

Going International: The experience of smaller companies overseas, G D Newbould, P J Buckley and J Thurwell, Associated Business Press (1978)

Selling, Importing and Exporting, Managing Your Business Guides, Hamlyn (1980)

The Strategy of Multinational Enterprise, M Z Brooke, Pitman (1978)

UK Companies Operating Overseas: Tax and financial strategies, Oyez Intelligence Report (1981)

10. PEOPLE

As your business expands, its needs for more people and people with different skills will increase.

The development of people within the business and their response to the challenges that growth offers will become of paramount importance. A business can go so far in developing its own people but there will come times when recruitment of new staff will become necessary.

What are the characteristics that the person must have to fulfil the job?

To answer this, you must have a specification of the job. The main features of a job description are set out later in this chapter. You can then use the job description to develop a description of the person you require. Perhaps this is the most difficult step. You are trying to imagine the perfect person for the position. Here are some of the key features of your description of the ideal person:

- age
- education
- qualifications
- experience
- intelligence
- motivation
- personality
- communicative skills
- appearance
- domestic circumstances
- languages and other skills.

Remember that your description must not only match the job but also the expected future development of it.

It is useful to highlight those requirements that are absolutely necessary to do the job well and place them in order of importance. Also identify those requirements that you could dispense with, as they are met by other people already within the business.

Imagine this description as your shopping list for recruitment. Having decided on your person, which method of recruitment should you use?

Methods of recruiting

Doing it yourself.   This implies not only that you know what type of person you want but also how to find them. It might appear to be cheaper than using agencies or other sources but it may not be if you count the cost of your time and the cost of advertising. Ask yourself also if you possess the interviewing skills required to identify whether the applicants match your shopping list. To do this effectively requires skill. Some businessmen are good at interviewing, particularly if they have been trained, but others are not. If the skills are not available internally, then consider using outside help.

Doing it yourself may depend largely upon the seniority of staff you wish to recruit. It may be that you are perfectly happy to recruit a young apprentice, but not a new sales director.

Using outside agencies and consultants.   If you recruit through an agency or consultant, take care to select the right one, depending on the level and experience of staff that you need. There is a vast difference between using a staff recruitment agency for clerical staff, executive selection agencies for middle management, and 'head hunters' for your top executives.

Staff recruitment agencies will usually cover the initial pre-selection of appropriate candidates. Their effectiveness in this process will depend on their knowledge of your organisation and your needs. Remember that each agency has a different position in the labour market. Some specialise in recruiting executive secretaries and others in junior typists. It pays to use a number of agencies, and build up your experience of their particular strengths.

Use executive selection agencies to find managers with particular skills and experience. They will undoubtedly ask you to specify precisely the person you want, their position in the organisation and future prospects. They may handle the advertising for you and should advise on publications for the person you want. They will do the initial interviews and shortlist those who are likely to be suitable.

'Head hunters' search out, through their contacts, individuals at high levels in business for key positions.

Establishing a pay structure

How should rates of pay be determined? Many businessmen would argue that market forces should suffice. This approach has the benefit of simplicity but is often short-sighted. If you pay just enough to keep your staff then sooner or later they will realise it. This basis also does not recognise the contribution individuals made to the success of the business. If efforts are not fairly rewarded then do not expect efforts. Remember also that a pay policy which is regarded as fair by your staff may help you to retain your staff during labour shortages. Sooner or later in your expansion you should establish a formal pay structure based on evaluation of jobs. As a guide this will be needed once you employ, say, fifty people.

In job evaluation you have to compare different types of skills which contribute in very different ways to the success of your business. How does the contribution of your sales representative compare to that of your production supervisor, or to the managing director's secretary? Some factors involved in job evaluation are:

● the level of responsibility

● the skills required

● the degree of supervision

● the conditions in which the job is carried out.

The degree of importance your business attaches to each of these factors has to be established. No doubt there are others, too. Although the process of evaluation can be carried out in what might appear to be a scientific manner, inevitably the end result will be your judgment. You will have to be satisfied that the results are not only fair but are also perceived to be fair by all your staff.

One difficult problem to solve is how the organisation should allow for appeals by those members of staff who feel badly treated. You should establish a system, otherwise problems could develop without your knowledge.

Trial periods and dismissal rules for new staff

After recruitment, it is important to review the performance of new staff. This is of course just sound management but there are legal reasons as well. The law requires certain periods of notice to be given before employment can be terminated. There are statutory minimum periods of notice, which in practice may be longer because of the particular terms of the employment contract. The basic rules, however, are that if your new recruit turns out to be unsatisfactory, you may terminate their employment without any minimum period of notice up to four weeks after their employment. After that initial period of four weeks' employment, you are required to give the following periods of notice:

● for periods of continuous employment of less than two years, not less than one week's notice

● for periods of continuous employment of more than two years, but less than twelve years, not less than one week's notice for each of those years of continuous employment

● for a period of continuous employment of twelve years or more, not less than twelve weeks' notice.

You can, however, dismiss an employee without notice in a case of gross misconduct warranting summary dismissal. There are some other exceptions to these rules but if you are in doubt, consult a lawyer.

By the end of the thirteenth week of employment, you are required to give a new employee either a contract of employment or a written statement incorporating the conditions of employment.

It is important to make the distinction between a contract and a written statement. This is because subsequently the statement can be changed unilaterally, either by yourself, or in the case of a dispute, by an industrial tribunal, whereas the contract cannot. You should seek legal advice on the wording of documents before their issue to employees.

The contract or statement of employment conditions must include:

● parties involved

● date when the employment commenced

● basis of computation of pay and when it falls due, i.e. weekly or monthly

● definition of hours to be worked

● holiday entitlement

● rules applied to sickness and sickness pay

● details of any pension scheme

● the period of notice

● the employee's job title

● the disciplinary rules

● the disciplinary rules affecting the employee

● the date of expiry, if applicable.

The trial periods to remember in the application of disciplinary procedures are:

● If the employment is terminated after 26 weeks' continuous service, an employee is entitled to request a written statement giving details of the reason for his dismissal. This statement must be given to the employee within fourteen days of his request.

● After 52 weeks of being continuously employed, an employee has the right not to be unfairly dismissed and if he is dismissed can complain to an industrial tribunal. 'Continuously employed' means working for sixteen hours or more per week. The same rights apply to those who have worked eight hours or more but less than sixteen hours per week for a period of five years or more. This applies to all companies who employ more than twenty people. For those companies employing less than twenty people, the relevant period of continuous employment is two years, as long as that company together with associates has not employed at any time more than twenty people in that two-year period.

Once again there are exceptions to these rules and if you are in doubt, consult a lawyer.

Job descriptions

Do you know what your job is? Most people think they do but it is surprising how difficult it is to write it down. This can, however, be a revealing exercise, since the perception employees have of their own jobs often differs considerably from the management's view. In a period of expansion, jobs evolve more quickly and the disparity quickly leads to false expectations and disappointments for both staff and management. It is a good idea to establish job descriptions and, initially at least, the employee should write it.

This also provides an occasion to review how each individual spends his time.

Set out below are the main features of a typical job description:

- job title
- immediate superior
- where the job is based, its location and division or department
- the main objectives of the job
- the staff who are to be supervised, including, if appropriate, an organisation chart
- specific responsibilities in detail. It is often useful to define those of the superior or subordinates and equals as well, to ensure that a clear picture is obtained of what is actually involved
- main reporting and working relationships
- levels of authority and size of budgets to be controlled, if applicable
- accountability, including frequency and to whom
- responsibility for any of the company's assets
- performance criteria and by whom the performance will be appraised.

Appraisal meetings and action plans

The job description should be agreed by an appropriate person of authority in the company. Regular and predetermined appraisal meetings should be arranged, at which the responsibilities, as outlined in the job

79

description, are compared with current experience. The targets for the immediate future should be set and those of the immediate past compared with actual performance. Significant achievements should be recognised.

By this means, constructive action plans can be adopted for each individual, so that they can develop and increase their usefulness to the organisation and also obtain greater personal satisfaction and reward.

Remuneration of employees

The principal elements in motivating management and staff revolves around skills such as leadership and communication. Nevertheless, the remuneration paid and the form it takes is important.

Basic salary.   Should there be a grading scheme which implies job evaluation? This may be more fair but can lead to inflexibility. It also involves administrative effort and may not be viable in smaller companies.

Total cost v composition.   The employer is largely concerned with the total cost to him of each employee and the return he gets on that investment. How that total cost is made up is largely irrelevant, unless any of the elements involve particularly onerous administration costs or tie up capital.

Due to the vagaries of the UK tax system, the employee can benefit significantly by the arrangement of the elements within the total package. An employer can therefore substantially improve the worth of a package to an employee without increasing the cost to himself as an employer.

Bonus schemes.   The idea is to relate earnings to effort. It is easier to achieve with direct production workers and sales staff than with production, overhead and administrative staff.

Bonus schemes can be related to individual or group performance. Individual schemes provide a more direct incentive but can lead to unwillingness to help others and therefore can have a divisive effect. Group schemes promote team spirit but run into problems if some members of the group fail to pull their weight.

Great care needs to be exercised in commencing a bonus scheme because once it is in operation it is difficult to change.

Discretionary bonuses provide greater flexibility but are open to charges of favouritism.

Employees suffer income tax under PAYE on bonuses.

Share incentive schemes.   A share of the equity is an easily understood incentive for employees. Growth in net assets and earnings of the business can be seen to lead directly to an increase in the wealth of the employee. Since dividends are usually very small or non-existent from fast growing private companies, a share of the equity is of limited value unless it can be realised. It is therefore important that the owner and minority shareholder initially agree the circumstances and basis of conversion of the equity into cash. It is also important to decide the proportion of the equity to give to the employee.

In devising a share incentive scheme, it is necessary to consider whether the executive should purchase shares outright or be granted options to acquire shares in the future. In both cases, the incentive is still the prospect of a profit from the shares as the value of the company increases.

The appeal of the option method is that no immediate cash outlay is required. It does suffer, however, from the tax disadvantage that when the option is exercised any increase in the value of the shares over the option price is liable to income tax. Only subsequent increases in value are treated as capital gains.

The straight purchase of shares by the employee at full market value does not normally result in any charge to income tax and future increases in value will be treated as capital gains. The problem is funding the purchase. Money may be borrowed from the bank or possibly from the company itself, provided the employee is not a director. However, interest paid on such borrowings will only be allowed for tax if the company is 'close' for tax purposes (basically under the control of five or fewer shareholders) and the employee has five per cent or more of the share capital or works for the greater part of his time in the company.

Any attempt to reduce the price of the shares, and hence the funding problem, by attaching restrictions to them, will result in unpleasant tax consequences for the employee. Income tax will automatically be charged on any increase in value of the shares at the end of seven years from the date of purchase or before if the restrictions are removed or the executive disposes of the shares. It should be noted that restrictions are widely defined by the taxing statutes and include the pledging of the shares as security for borrowings in certain circumstances. On the brighter side, shares offered to employees are normally small minority holdings in unquoted companies, so that it is often possible to agree a very low value for tax purposes; normally much lower than the proprietor thinks the shares are worth. For this reason, and because the future growth in the value of the shares is generally treated as a capital gain, outright share purchase is generally to be recommended.

Profit-sharing and SAYE share options.   In recent years, there have been two moves to encourage wider share ownership by executives and employees. The first was in 1978 with 'profit-sharing schemes'. These permit a company to contribute money into a trust fund which is then used to acquire shares in the company for the benefit of employees. The second was in 1980 with the introduction of SAYE (Save As You Earn) share option schemes. Under these schemes employees are given an option to buy shares at not less than 90% of the current market value. The

81

shares have to be bought from the proceeds of SAYE savings contracts.

Tax advantages are granted to participants in the schemes but both suffer from two disadvantages. First, the schemes must be open to all full-time employees of five years' standing or more in order to obtain Inland Revenue approval. Second, there are low limits on the value of shares that may be acquired. Under a profit-sharing scheme, the maximum value of shares that may be acquired by the trustees for the benefit of employees is £1,250 p.a.. The maximum contribution that may be paid under a SAYE savings contract is £600 p.a. for five years.

In most cases, therefore, these schemes will be too inflexible for the expanding private company and are not dealt with further in this book.

Cars.   A car scheme may be a major benefit to an employee because he not only saves on running costs but also need not find the capital cost for initial purchase. The tax rules are complicated but generally any tax payable by the employee would be less than if the value of the benefit were paid to him in cash.

On the other hand, company cars do involve fairly heavy administration cost and they can tie up capital, thus costing money via interest.

Subsidised mortgages.   These are common only in financial institutions. A major advantage of a subsidised mortgage scheme can be the degree of dependence which the employee must place on the company.

A qualifying period may be applied but this can be a problem in hiring new staff if they already have a mortgage with their existing employer.

Pension schemes.   Due to the inadequacy of the state pension scheme, many employers provide a private scheme. Most employers contract out of the state scheme, though the trend in recent Budgets has made this course less attractive.

Small firms may not be able to justify a group scheme of their own but can still enable employees to participate in a private pension arrangement through individual schemes operated by insurance companies.

The attractions of company pension schemes vary greatly from one employee to another. Women who intend to have a family rather than a career are unlikely to be interested. Due to the current situation on transferability, younger men who do not expect to stay with their current employer for life may also see the value of a company scheme as questionable. Older employees who do intend to stay with an employer for the rest of their working life, on the other hand, may value a pension extremely highly.

The cost of providing a worthwhile pension for a man in his 50's may be a strong disincentive to hiring him.

Schemes may be contributory or non-contributory. The latter either cost the employer more or provide lower benefits.

Pension payments by the employee are generally deductible from his income for calculating income tax.

Life assurance schemes.   These are usually linked to pension schemes and based on a multiple of salary which tends to be kept in line with what competitors in the labour market are providing.

Long-term disability schemes.   A worthwhile benefit which does not cost much to provide.

Private medical insurance.   An increasingly popular benefit. Higher-paid employees do get taxed on this benefit but there is still an advantage in the group rates which employers can obtain.

Subsidised meals.   These can have quite a high cash value. There are also less tangible benefits where local eating facilities are either distant, non-existent or overcrowded. The opportunity for people to get together over lunch may be a further advantage and on-site facilities may result in less time being taken away from work. Employers should, however, review the cost and administrative burden.

Staff discounts.   These are obviously limited to businesses producing consumer products and services. The cost to the company tends to be much less than the value to the employee.

Holidays.   These tend to be set at the norm of industry.

Season-ticket loans.   Season-ticket loans are of greater benefit to lower level staff.

Flexitime.   The benefits of flexitime need to be balanced against the administration costs and the disruption caused by not having everyone available at the same time.

Notice period.   Long periods are of greater advantage to the employee than employer. It is difficult to make an employee work out a long notice period against his will.

A people checklist

1. Ask yourself if you have been and still are developing the people your business needs to fulfil your expansion plans.   ☐

2. Review your plans for the future utilisation and current development of people and ensure that adequate priority will be given to this aspect of the management of your business, despite the other pressures expansion may bring.   ☐

3. Ensure that adequate job descriptions are established in consultation with the people involved. Do all your people know what is expected of them, how it will be monitored and how this may change as the business develops? ☐

4. Ask yourself if you are getting the best out of your people and if they are getting the best out of their job. Consider establishing a formal system of individual appraisal at which performance can be reviewed and specific action plans developed for the benefit of both the business and the individual. ☐

5. Ask yourself if your pay structure, including incentives and bonuses, is fair and is seen to be fair and consistent by your staff. What will happen when the business expands? It may be that a formal system of job evaluation will be needed. ☐

6. Have you identified your anticipated staff turnover and your recruitment needs? Are your procedures adequate to meet them? Ensure that your recruitment process includes:

   ● accurate job definition ☐
   ● realistic specification of the right person ☐
   ● appropriate selection procedures. ☐

7. Ensure that the legal aspects of your personnel policies are properly dealt with, particularly in relation to:

   ● trial periods and dismissal ☐
   ● contracts of employment ☐
   ● pension arrangements. ☐

8. Remember that people are a major asset. Expansion may be good for the business, but it should be seen as an opportunity for the people too. Don't take them for granted. ☐

Further action to be taken by me

1.

2.

3.

4.

5.

6.

Where to go for further help

Organisations

Company Pensions Information Centre
7 Old Park Lane, London W1Y 3LJ
Tel: 01-493 4757

Department of Employment
Caxton House, Tothill St., London SW1H 9NA
Tel: 01-213 3000

Institute of Personnel Management
JPM House, Camp Rd., Wimbledon, London SW19
Tel: 01-946 9100

Manpower Services Commission, Corporate Services Division
Selkirk House, 166 High Holborn, London WC1V 6PF
Tel: 01-836 1213

National Association of Pension Funds
Sunley House, Bedford Park, Croydon CR0 0XY
Tel: 01-681 2017

Books

A Handbook of Salary Administration, M Armstrong and H Murlis, Kogan Page (1980)

Company Administration Handbook, Gower (5th ed, 1982): Part 5 The Company and its Employees

Corporate Manpower Planning, A R Smith (editor), Gower (1980)

Cost Effective Personnel Decisions, J Cannon, Institute of Personnel Management (1979)

Croner's Reference Book for Employers

Dismissal, R Upex, Sweet & Maxwell (1980)

Effective Interviewing for Employment Selection, C T Goodworth, Business Books (1979)

Employee Benefits and Incentive Rewards, Duncan

Employee Communications in the 1980s – A Personnel Manager's Guide, M Bland, Kogan Page (1980)

Employee Remuneration and Profit Sharing, R Greenhill, Woodhead-Faulkner (1980)

Employment Contract, I Smith, Sweet & Maxwell (1980)

Employment Interviewing, J Munro Fraser, Macdonald & Evans (5th ed, 1978)

Employment Law Manual, D Payne (editor), Gower

Executive and all Employee Share Schemes, Tony Vernon-Harcourt, Monks Publications (1981)

Fringe Benefits, J F Staddon, London Chamber of Commerce & Industry (1982)

Handbook on Pensions and Employee Benefits – their provision and administration, Kluwer

Hepple and O'Higgins Employment Law, Sweet & Maxwell (1981)

How To Be Your Own Personnel Manager, P Humphrey, Institute of Personnel Management (1981)

How to Recruit, R Braithwaite and P Schofield, Gower (1979)

Job Evaluation – Objectives and Methods, G Thornmason, Institute of Personnel Management (1981)

National Analysis of Salaries and Wages, Reward (1982)

New Encyclopaedia of Employment Law and Practice, Centurion Publications

Occupational Pensions, I Smith, Sweet and Maxwell (1980)

Office Salaries Analysis 1982, Institute of Administrative Management

Pay Systems: Principles and Techniques, R H S Beachans, Heinemann and Society of Company and Commercial Accountants (1979)

Pension Schemes: A Guide to Principles and Practice, M Pilch and V Wood Gower (1979)

Pensions – a practical guide, Oyez Practice Notes, Oyez (1980)

Practical Manpower Planning, J Bramham, Institute of Personnel Management (1978)

Practical Participation and Involvement: Vol 1 Communication in Practice, Institute of Personnel Management (1981)

Selwyn's Law of Employment, Butterworth (3rd ed, 1980)

Survey of Fringe Benefits for Office Staff, 1982, Alfred Marks Statistical Services Division

The ABC of Interviewing, M Higham, Institute of Personnel Management (1979)

The Complete Guide to Managing Your Business, Eaglemoss Publications: Ch 6 Employees and your relations with them, and Ch 12 Pensions

Union Members, G Morris, Sweet and Maxwell (1980)

Wages & Salaries, G R Rubin, Sweet and Maxwell (1980)

CONCLUSION

This kit was written with thoughts of the end of the recession in our minds. We hope that these thoughts will become reality and prefer to be optimistic about it. The signs are not clear, however, and the longer the recession continues, the more plausible the prophets of doom become. Nevertheless, there is even now a wide range of performance between different businesses and some are very successful. We believe that their success owes much to sound management and that is what this kit is about.

The Tolley Subscriber Service

The benefits to you are . . .

Free service
No extra cost to you.

Up-to-date books
You need never again run the risk of using out-of-date editions.

Finance Bill Memorandum
Sent to you, *free of charge,* soon after each Finance Bill is published.

Pre-publication prices
You will be able to purchase most new titles at introductory discounts.

Reduced subscriptions
Tolley's business periodicals, Partnership Management, Company Secretary's Review, Tolley's Practical Tax and Finance Director's Review are obtainable at specially reduced rates for Tolley Subscribers.

Reduced conference fees
You will be entitled to reductions in fees for Tolley conferences.

Annual confirmation
Each year we will write to you with details of your standing order. Only after you have confirmed your requirements will the book(s) be sent to you. You may also vary your order at any other time.

Free Postage
Only books on standing order will be sent post-free in the United Kingdom and Eire.

Time-saving and convenient
The next edition of books on your standing order are sent to you automatically upon publication.

Become a Tolley Subscriber by placing a standing order for the next edition of any Tolley publication.

Tolley's Practical Business Periodicals

All Tolley periodicals are sent by first class post. Each is supplied with frequent cumulative indexes, which, together with the free binders, convert single issues into updated valuable reference works to use again and again. All include free supplements from time to time on important topics such as Finance Bills and Acts. *New subscribers may cancel their subscriptions within eight weeks and obtain a full refund.*

Partnership Management

This twelve page monthly is devoted exclusively to practical information and guidance for partnerships, partners and those advising them. It contains articles and news on every aspect of partnership management (including personal aspects where appropriate) from taxation to staff recruitment, plus legal and parliamentary notes and regular features on provision for retirement and office technology. A special feature is In Practice, highlighting particular points of law and practice and giving advice on problem-solving. A quarterly cumulative index and a ring binder are supplied for easy reference.

Annual Subscription £40.00; All Tolley Subscribers £36.00.

Company Secretary's Review

An eight page practical business fortnightly that covers the entire field of work of the modern company secretary/administrator: company law, accounting, employment, taxation, health and safety, insurance, energy, national insurance, export, EEC, pensions, transport, property, etc. Concise news items plus sources of further information, detailed topical articles, law reports with commentary, advance warning of key dates and many other regular features, combine to produce a uniquely practical updating service. It is indexed every four issues; a storage binder is supplied for easy reference.

Annual Subscription £49.00; All Tolley Subscribers and ICSA Members £39.20.

Finance Director's Review

This eight page fortnightly is designed specifically for senior financial executives. It records the latest changes in the world of corporate finance, raising finance, cash management, insurance, accounting, pensions, taxation, property, investment, export, etc., plus news of the latest economic indicators. Regular columns analyse the gilt-edged market, company performance, foreign exchange and UK and overseas interest rates. Articles examine both technical details and practical problems. As with all Tolley fortnightlies, it is indexed every four issues and a storage binder is supplied for easy reference.

Annual Subscription £55.00; Tolley and TPT Subscribers £49.50; CSR Subscribers £41.25

Tolley's Practical Tax

A fortnightly, eight page bulletin that concentrates solely on taxation matters for the busy accountant and taxation practitioner. It covers all United Kingdom direct and indirect taxes (except Customs duties) and includes all the latest statutes and regulations, statements of practice, concessions, cases, treaties and official publications. Worked examples and articles by leading authors explain new developments and our 'Points of Practice' series gives valuable information that really is unobtainable elsewhere.

Annual Subscription £45.00; CSR and FDR Subscribers £31.50; Tolley Subscribers £38.25.

Tolley Book List

Tax Annuals

Tolley's tax annuals are widely used as the work of first reference by thousands of practitioners. Each is fully revised every year.

Annual Reference Guides

The special features of each include: ☐clear, comprehensive, concise explanation of the law ☐chapters in alphabetical order ☐references throughout to relevant statutes, case law, Inland Revenue statements, etc. and to related sections elsewhere in the annuals ☐comprehensive index ☐table of statutes ☐distinctive cover for quick identification ☐carefully designed, readable text.

Tolley's Income Tax 1982/83
By Eric L Harvey FCA
512pp   ISBN 0 85459 074-9   **£9.95**

Tolley's Corporation Tax 1982/83
By Glyn Saunders MA
320pp   ISBN 0 85459 075-7   **£7.50**

Tolley's Capital Gains Tax 1982/83
By David Harrington MA (Oxon) FCA and
Glyn Saunders MA
284pp   ISBN 0 85459 076-5   **£8.75**

Tolley's Capital Transfer Tax 1982/83
By Robert Wareham BSc (Econ) FCA and
Christopher Greene FCA
216pp   ISBN 0 85459 077-3   **£7.95**

Tolley's Taxation in the Republic of Ireland 1982/83
By Glyn Saunders MA and
Eric L Harvey FCA ATII
224pp   ISBN 0 85459 081-1   **£7.95**

Tolley's Taxation in the Channel Islands & Isle of Man 1982
By David Harrington MA (Oxon) FCA
184pp   ISBN 0 85459 064-1   **£6.95**

Other Annuals

Tolley's Tax Tables 1982/83
16pp   ISBN 0 85459 065-X   **£2.50**

Tolley's Tax Cases 1982
By Victor Grout CBE LLB
435pp   ISBN 0 85459 061-7   **£10.75**

Tolley's Tax Data 1982/83
By Robert Wareham BSc (Econ) FCA and
David Harrington MA (Oxon) FCA
80pp   ISBN 0 85459 068-4   **£3.95**

Tolley's Tax Planning 1982/83
Edited by A L Chapman LLB FTII
800pp   ISBN 0 85459 089-7   **£17.50**

Grout's Value Added Tax Cases
By Victor Grout CBE LLB
264pp   ISBN 0 85459 046-3   **£10.75**

Tolley's Tax Cards 1982/83
Compiled by G V Hart FTII
36pp   ISBN 0 85459 078-1   **£7.95**

Tolley's Tax Computations 1982/83
By Thomson McLintock & Co
Loose-leaf with service.
ISBN 0 85459 079-X   **£35.00**

Taxwise Taxation Workbook 1982/83
By Arnold Homer FCA ATII, Rita Burrows
ACIS ATII and Peter Gravestock FCA ATII
472pp   ISBN 0 85459 083-8   **£10.75**

Taxwise Capital Transfer Tax Workbook 1982/83
By Arnold Homer FCA ATII, Rita Burrows
ACIS ATII and Peter Gravestock FCA ATII
232pp   ISBN 0 85459 084-6   **£7.95**

Other Tax Books

Finance Act 1982 Annotated
352pp   ISBN 0 85459 072-2   **£11.50**

Jersey: A Low-Tax Area
By Mark Solly FCA ATII
336pp   Paperback
ISBN 0 85459 054-4   **£15.00**
Hardback
ISBN 0 85459 053-6   **£18.00**

Tolley's Taxation in Gibraltar 1982
By James Levy LLB and
Simon Caplan FCA FTII
165pp   ISBN 0 85459 044-7   **£8.50**

Tolley's Development Land Tax 4th Edition
By Robert W Maas FCA
256pp   ISBN 0 85459 056-0   **£10.50**

Tolley's Double Taxation Relief
By Deloitte Haskins and Sells
175pp   ISBN 0 510 49387-4   **£7.95**

Tolley's Stamp Duties 2nd Edition
By Sheila V Masters LLB FCA ATII
136pp   ISBN 0 510 49024-7   **£5.95**

Tolley's Stock Relief
By Glyn Saunders MA
49pp   ISBN 0 85459 052-8   **£3.50**

Tolley's US/UK Double Tax Treaty
By Arthur Andersen & Co
212pp   ISBN 0 510 49421-8   **£9.95**

Sotinwa's Nigerian Tax Handbook 1982
By G A Sotinwa FCA
251pp   ISBN 0 85459 055-2   **£11.50**

Company Law

Tolley's Companies Act 1981
By George Eccles and Jenny Cox
400pp   Paperback
    ISBN 0 85459 039-0   **£7.95**
    Hardback
    ISBN 0 85459 058-7   **£11.95**

Tolley's Companies Act 1980
By Mary Arden and George Eccles
291pp   Paperback
    ISBN 0 510 49415-3   **£6.95**
    Hardback
    ISBN 0 85459 059-5   **£11.95**

†**Tolley's Company Law**
Edited by A L Chapman LLB FTII
pp tba   ISBN 0 85459 069-2   **£ tba**

Tolley's Index to Companies Legislation
Compiled by Josephine Stafford BA
74pp   ISBN 0 85459 067-6   **£3.95**

Employment Law

†**Tolley's Health and Safety at Work Handbook**
Edited by Malcolm Dewis LLB
pp tba   ISBN 0 85459 029-3   **£11.50**

**Tolley's Employment Handbook 2nd Edition
with 1980 Supplement**
By Elizabeth Slade MA (Oxon)
276pp   ISBN 0 510 49390-4   **£8.95**

Social Security

Tolley's Social Security and State Benefits
By Jim Matthewman and Nigel Lambert
448pp   ISBN 0 85459 027-7   **£8.95**

Insolvency

†**Liquidation Manual**
By Paul Shewell MA FCA and
John Powell FCA
pp tba   ISBN 0 85459 028-5   **£21.00**

†**Receivership Manual 2nd Edition**
By Donald Chilvers FCA and
Paul Shewell MA FCA
pp tba   ISBN 0 85459 070-6   **£ tba**

**Employees' Rights in Receiverships
and Liquidations**
By Guy T E Parsons and William F Ratford
208pp   ISBN 0 510 49396-3   **£14.95**

Accounting

Companies Accounts Check List No. 1
By Peat Marwick Mitchell & Co   **£4.20 + VAT**
24pp   ISBN 0 85459 073-0   **(per pack of 5)**

Companies Accounts Check List No. 2
By Peat Marwick Mitchell & Co   **£4.20 + VAT**
32pp   ISBN 0 85459 066-8   **(per pack of 5)**

Tolley's CCA Conversion Kit
By Michael Kirwan and John Belton
229pp   ISBN 0 85459 016-1   **£45.00 + VAT**

Tolley's Reporting under CCA
By Peat Marwick Mitchell & Co
275pp   ISBN 0 85459 048-X   **£18.00**

Miscellaneous

†**Tolley's Expansion Kit for Business**
By Touche Ross & Co
pp tba   ISBN 0 85459 071-4   **£ tba**

Tolley's Survival Kit for Small Businesses
By Touche Ross & Co
43pp   ISBN 0 85459 040-4   **£2.95**
    Eire Version
    ISBN 0 85459 051-X   **£3.50**

Tolley's European Community Institutions
By Joanne S Foakes BA (Oxon)
83pp   ISBN 0 85459 060-9   **£4.50**

**Tolley's Profit Sharing and other
Share Acquisition Schemes
with 1980 Supplement**
By Francis G Sandison BCL MA (Oxon)
231pp   ISBN 0 510 49383-1   **£9.95**

The Independent Director
By R I Tricker MA FCA FCMA
104pp   ISBN 0 510 49378-5   **£4.50**

CSR Survey of Company Car Schemes
By Jill Greatorex
115pp   ISBN 0 85459 038-2   **£15.00**

†**CSR Survey of Employee Benefits**
By William M Mercer Benefits Ltd
pp tba   ISBN 0 85459 088-9   **£ tba**

 Tolley on Prestel

Regularly updated information for business
users can be found on Tolley's Prestel Pages.
Frames include: retail price index, details of
tax and social security rates, bank and
building society rates and the all stocks index.

Tolley on 551

†To be published shortly.

ORDER FORM

To: Tolley Publishing Co. Ltd.,
209 High Street, Croydon, Surrey CR0 1QR Telephone: 01-686 9141

Please supply the following publications now (or as soon as published):—

Title	Price each	Current Editions No.	£	Future Editions No.	
Tolley's Income Tax 1982/83	£9.95				IT82
Tolley's Corporation Tax 1982/83	£7.50				CT82
Tolley's Capital Gains Tax 1982/83	£8.75				CG82
Tolley's Capital Transfer Tax 1982/83	£7.95				CTT82
Tolley's Taxation in the Republic of Ireland 1982/83	£7.95				R182
Tolley's Tax Data 1982/83	£3.95				TTD82
Tolley's Tax Tables 1982/83	£2.50				TT82
Tolley's Tax Cases 1982	£10.75				TC82
Tolley's Taxation in the Channel Islands & IoM 1982	£6.95				C182
Tolley's Tax Planning 1982/83	£17.50				TP82
Grout's Value Added Tax Cases	£10.75				VATC
Tolley's Tax Cards 1982/83	£7.95				TXC82
Tolley's Tax Computations 1982/83	£35.00				TTC82
Finance Act 1982 Annotated	£11.50				FA82
Jersey: A Low-Tax Area Paperback edition	£15.00				JLT
Hardback edition	£18.00				JLTHB
Tolley's Taxation in Gibraltar 1982	£8.50				G182
Tolley's Development Land Tax 4th Edition	£10.50				DLT82
Tolley's Double Taxation Relief	£7.95				DTR82
Tolley's Stamp Duties 2nd Edition	£5.95				SD80
Tolley's Stock Relief	£3.50				SR81
Tolley's US/UK Double Tax Treaty	£9.95				DTT80
Tolley's Companies Act 1981 Paperback edition	£7.95				CO81
Hardback edition	£11.95				COH81
Tolley's Companies Act 1980 Paperback edition	£6.95				CO80
Hardback edition	£11.95				COH80
Tolley's Company Law	£ tba				TCL
Tolley's Index to Companies Legislation	£3.95				ICL
Tolley's Health and Safety at Work Handbook	£11.50				HSW
Tolley's Employment Handbook 2nd Edition with 1980 Supplement	£8.95				E&S80
Tolley's Social Security and State Benefits	£8.95				TSS80
Liquidation Manual	£21.00				LM80
Receivership Manual 2nd Edition	£ tba				RM82
Employees' Rights in Receiverships and Liquidations	£14.95				ERR79
Companies Accounts Check List No. 1 pack of 5	£4.83 ‡				CAC1
No. 2 pack of 5	£4.83 ‡				CAC2
Tolley's CCA Conversion Kit	£51.75 ‡				CCAKT
Tolley's Reporting under CCA	£18.00				RCCA
Tolley's Expansion Kit for Business	£ tba				TEK
Tolley's Survival Kit for Small Businesses	£2.95				TSK
Tolley's Business — a Survival Kit (Eire Version)	£3.50				ITSK
Tolley's European Community Institutions	£4.50				ECI
Tolley's Profit Sharing and other Share Acquisition Schemes with 1980 Supplement	£9.95				P&S80
CSR Survey of Company Car Schemes	£15.00				CCS80
CSR Survey of Employee Benefits	£ tba				SEB
Taxwise Taxation Workbook 1982/83	£10.75				TTW1
Taxwise Capital Transfer Tax Workbook	£7.95				TCTW1

Please add 5% for post & packing*

Cheque enclosed for total amount of order   £ _____

Name _____ Tel. No: _____

Firm _____

Address_____

_____ Postcode_____

Signed _____ Date _____

Registered No. 729731 England VAT No. 243 3583 67

001 A B C D E

*Post and packing charges waived if books are placed on Standing Order, under the Tolley Subscriber service.   ‡Inclusive of VAT @ 15%.